Mentor me

Share the Joy of Mentoring for the Lord

by

Betty Bender

Brenda Birckholtz

Becky Blackmon

Judy Cofer

Martha Coletta

Laura Dayton

Publishing Designs, Inc.
P.O. Box 3241
Huntsville, Alabama 35810

© 2020 Publishing Designs, Inc.

Cover and page design: CrosslinCreative.net

Editor: Peggy Coulter

Printed in the United States

Publisher's Cataloging-in-Publication Data

Mentor Me

166 pp.

13 chapters and study questions

ISBN 978-0-9755962-2-7 (alk. paper)

1. Christian women—Mentoring. 2. Relationship skills—awareness, listening, research.

3. Women—married, single, daughter-in-law, mother-in-law, widow, caregiver.

I. Title.

248.8

Lovingly dedicated

in memory of Betty Bender and Lea Fowler

Ageless servants of God whose influence lives on to
promote faith for a lifetime and whose teaching continues
to guide many in the way of eternal life.

Not unto us, O Lord, not unto us, but to Your name give glory,
Because of Your mercy, because of your truth.
—Psalm 115:1 NKJV

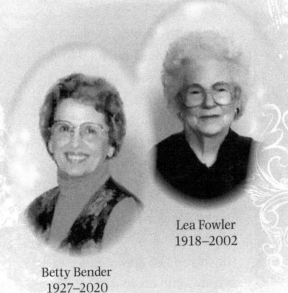

Lea Fowler
1918–2002

Betty Bender
1927–2020

Meet the Authors

by Brenda Birckholtz

Betty Bender, Columbia, Tennessee

Betty is our "good soil" girl. "Other seed fell into the good soil, and grew up, and produced a crop a hundred times as great" (Luke 8:8).

Betty decided at a very young age to take advantage of every opportunity the Lord put in her path to serve Him. From this heart of good soil God brought forth a hundred-fold harvest of good deeds that blessed countless people.

Brenda Birckholtz, Lithia, Florida

Brenda is our modern-day Barnabas, an encourager. When you meet and speak with Brenda, you will know right away that you have met someone who is genuinely interested in your well-being, wanting to respond in a most loving and thoughtful way. "Therefore encourage one another, and build up one another, just as you also are doing" (1 Thessalonians 5:11 ESV).

Becky Blackmon, Hewitt, Texas

Becky is our Ezra girl: "For Ezra had set his heart to study the law of the Lord and to practice it, and to teach His statutes and ordinances in Israel" (Ezra 7:10). Becky, a well-known author and speaker, will often tell us we need to learn, learn, learn, so we can grow, grow, grow, so we can change, change, change.

Judy Cofer, Columbia, Tennessee

Judy is our hospitality girl: "Let love of the brethren continue. Do not neglect to show hospitality to strangers, for by this some have entertained angels without knowing it" (Hebrews 13:1–2). As we meet annually for Bible study at Judy's house, she makes us feel like she has the honor of hosting us. That's real hospitality.

Martha Coletta, Clifton Park, New York

Marty is a wise woman. She is our "gentle and quiet" girl: "But let it be the hidden person of the heart, with the imperishable quality of a gentle and quiet spirit, which is precious in the sight of God" (1 Peter 3:4). When people meet Marty, they experience her gentleness and acceptance.

Laura Dayton, Harrodsburg, Kentucky

Laura is our nonconformist girl: "Therefore I urge you, brethren, by the mercies of God, to present your bodies a living and holy sacrifice, acceptable to God, which is your spiritual service of worship. And do not be conformed to this world, but be transformed by the renewing of your mind, so that you may prove what the will of God is, that which is good and acceptable and perfect" (Romans 12:1–2). As a new Christian in 1978, she stated that she was "pulling out all the stops" in her new life with God, and she did.

Not to us, O Lord,
Not to us,
But to Your name give glory
Because of Your lovingkindness,
Because of Your truth.

—Psalm 115:1

Contents

Introduction

Mentoring the Generations: Our Mission

A beautiful hymn titled "Faith of Our Fathers" heralds a message needed today. Mentoring each generation in the faith we hold dear is always needed and is urgent. Common observation may not tell the full story regarding the commitment, purity, passion, and knowledge that must be restored to every generation. We may look good on the surface, yet the sad statistics reveal a great decline in the number of young women engaged in true discipleship and Christian service. It is time to awaken the commitment among our sisterhood to the vital work of involvement and mentoring.

Jesus once asked a very important question: "When the Son of Man comes will He really find faith on the earth?" (Luke 18:8 NKJV). Contextually His audience consisted of the ever-quarrelsome Pharisees and His own disciples. In verse 33, the Lord's statement, "after they have scourged Him, they will kill Him, and the third day He will rise again," was designed to wake them up to be ready for His return. Jesus makes it crystal clear that the level of commitment required to enter life eternal requires a life totally dedicated to God. What can we understand from His powerful words?

Clearly the faith of our fathers involves far more than attending worship services and Bible study. Jesus calls His disciples to a life that puts following Him and fulfilling His plan and purpose as the absolute number one commitment of our lives.

Mentor Me seeks to awaken the important work of teaching, demonstrating, and becoming lovingly involved in the lives of our sisters. That involvement is called *mentoring*.

In her final days Sister Edna Pigman, who mentored many women over her ninety-two-year lifetime, wrote these inspiring words:

We, as Christian women today, need to be an influence for good. Our perseverance, faith, and steadfastness may be the only example that someone around us needs to turn her life around.

Her home was a hub for young women to come, be loved, and receive instruction. Her life was a flame of faithfulness and love for the Lord's church and work.

How about us?

How *Mentor Me* Began

Six women gathered for a long weekend in 2014 to draw closer to God through studying the Bible. It was a connect-meeting for some and a reunion for others. But they all had one friend in common—Betty Bender, their mentor.

The idea evolved to begin work on a book about mentoring. The process became a annual tradition, and it took five consecutive years for them to shout "Finished!"

A common sentiment prevailed: "To be honest, I never think of myself as a mentor because I need so much mentoring." Another way of saying this is, "The best teacher is always a student."

Top L to R:

Brenda Birckholtz,
Betty Bender,
Becky Blackmon

Bottom L to R:
Martha Coletta,
Laura Dayton,
Judy Cofer

Betty Bender went to be with the Lord on February 14, 2020, at the age of ninety-two. Betty would have loved to have seen this book published and held it in her hands, but even better, she inspired the book!

Mother of three, grandmother of seven, great-grandmother of nineteen, preacher's wife, and elder's wife, Betty Bender was a teacher of preachers' wives at the Northeast School of Biblical Studies in New York. She authored five books and co-authored this book. Betty conducted marriage and evangelistic workshops through the United States and made several international mission trips. She often stated, "I wake up each day determined to bring everyone I meet a little closer to the Lord." Her pattern was Psalm 37:4: "Delight yourself in the Lord and He will give you the desires of your heart."

Chapter 1

Mentor Me, I'm the Mentor

by Betty Bender

It All Began with Bible Study

We see some examples in the New Testament of Jesus taking a few of His disciples off to study and pray together. Jesus did not instruct us to follow that pattern, but His example proves its benefit.

In the first few years of our married life, Duane and I grew together spiritually enough that we began to have "a hungering and thirsting" for deeper understanding of the Scriptures. We asked a few couples to our house one evening to open the Bible and search the Scriptures together to learn more about the message in God's Word as the Bereans did (Acts 17:11). We decided that night to make it a weekly gathering, so for a number of months we studied in this small group. Through this experience, we saw the value of small discussion groups. Since then, every place we lived, we got a small group together to study the Bible with us.

One fall after we went to New England, when the men were having their retreat at Ganderbrook, Maine, I called Lea Fowler, a preacher's wife, and boldly asked if I could come to her home in Fryeburg, Maine, and study with her on some subject we had previously talked about studying together. Lea graciously invited me to come, so we spent two days studying deeply on a selected biblical subject.

The next fall during the men's Ganderbrook Retreat, Lea invited Fran Carpenter and me to come to her house to study another subject. Fran wanted

Judith Merriam,
Betty Bender,
Lea Fowler,
Fran Carpenter

to bring Judith Merriam along, so Lea consented. That is how it all began. We went to Lea's home and spent the night. We studied all day, enjoyed a good meal together, went to bed, and got up the next morning, eager to study some more. We convened several more times at Lea's in Fryeburg, Maine, later at Fran's in Tilton, New Hampshire, and then at my house in Methuen, Massachusetts.

It was such a joy for us to have time together to study God's Word. We decided we needed to do it more often, so for several years, we met together at one of our homes and had a good time studying and praying together, usually staying overnight and studying for part of two days. Then Duane and I moved to New York where we taught in the Northeast School of Biblical Studies. I taught the students' wives.

One year during the summer break, one of the students was not going home, so she asked to have a weekly Bible study with me. I had just finished reading *Disciplines of the Beautiful Woman* by Anne Ortlund, and she talked about ladies' small group Bible studies. So borrowing an idea from that book, I came up with an idea how to structure a small group study. I invited two of the other teachers, Marty Coletta and Laura (Quesada) Dayton to join me and this student in a study one evening each week for the summer.

Love Circles

At the beginning of the next school year, I asked that small group if they wanted to continue the weekly study, knowing how busy we would all be when school started. Laura Dayton, ingenious person that she is, spoke up and suggested that each of us invite three others and start a group ourselves. So we all agreed we would include others and share the joy. Laura then suggested that we call the study groups "Love Circles." We liked that name, so I made copies of the way we had structured our summer study. The four of us started a Love Circle in each of our homes.

After we finished whatever book we were studying, we would ask each participant, "Would you like to start a Love Circle in your home?" And many did just that. As the idea spread, we eventually had the majority of the ladies in the congregation enrolled in a Love Circle.

After we left school and moved to different locations, I started Love Circles in every congregation where I worshiped.

Mentoring Tips

Those who knew Betty Bender and benefited from her wise mentoring will certainly agree that the following life-principles are worthy of handing down to another generation.

Things I Learned from Betty
by Brenda Birckholtz

1. *Wake up every day with the goal of bringing every person you encounter closer to God.*

2. *Take on some work areas that are out of your comfort zone and see where God leads you.* Your participation in the body of Christ should not consist exclusively of areas you like and are easy for you. If you are asked to do an uncomfortable job, say yes. You will know in time if that is where God wants you to work.

3. *Persevere in disciplining your child even when you feel tired and discouraged.* Betty shared this with me after I expressed my frustration and exhaustion while disciplining our two-year-old. Betty reminded me that parenting is demanding and tiring. She said that two years from this time, our

child would be in school and I would lose some of my influence in his life. That wisdom redirected my thinking.

4. *Speak first when someone appears to be shunning you.* Be the first to say, "Hello. How are you?" Let your warmth and acceptance break down walls that have been erected.

5. *Approach each aspect of life with God as your pilot.* "I just want to do what the Lord wants me to do. I'm just waiting for Him to show me the way." Betty's book, *Oh, Randle My Son, My Son,* demonstrates how she incorporated this into her life.

6. *Focus your mind on others, on their burdens, if you are weary and heavy laden.* This will lighten your load and bring you closer to God.

Passing the Baton: Brenda Birckholtz's Interview with Betty Bender

Brenda: What was the best part of your life?

Betty: Two times. (1) When the children were all in school, and we were active in a peaceful church in Tulsa, and (2) the last three years of Duane's life. The family was settled into a good life. Duane and I were in a good work, and we had a lovely home in Anderson, South Carolina.

— ✿ —

Brenda: What was the hardest part of your life?

Betty: When Randy was wandering the country, and we didn't know where he was. Many nights I lay awake in prayer, hoping he was safe.

— ✿ —

Brenda: What was your greatest victory?

Betty: Finishing college at seventy years of age. I had always wanted to go back to school, but I didn't want to neglect my work for the Lord to do so. When we moved to Anderson, South Carolina, I felt I would be able to carry on my work in the church and go to school too.

Brenda: What singular message would you give to preachers' wives, other wives, and mothers?

Betty: To preachers' wives: Choose your confidants with Christian women outside your congregation, i.e., nearby preachers' wives or friends from other congregations. As much as possible, be friends with all the women in the congregation without partiality.

To wives: Love your husband wholeheartedly. Put him first—before your children, before your friends, before your parents. The more you love him, the more thoughtful and loving he will be of you (Ephesians 5:22–25).

To mothers: Be a friend and a supporter but not a buddy. Your child will make buddies with his peers.

Brenda: What stages of grief did you go through when you lost your husband, Duane?

Betty: My grieving experience was different. I really didn't grieve until two years later. I was so busy trying to finish school so I could go to work, which was a necessity. I was two years away from a degree, so I rented a room to a college girl in order to stay in Anderson and finish school. Then I had to concentrate on moving to Columbia, Tennessee, and getting settled before school started at Columbia Academy where I went to work. I was so lonely the first winter in Columbia. I knew no one. Right away I started going to West Seventh church, and that helped me to get acquainted and make friends. Either Jewell Thomason or Pam Elder would always ask me to sit with them. Dorothy Jean Witherow and Laura Williams befriended me first, inviting me to go to a visitation meeting.

Brenda: What stages of grief did you go through when you lost your son Randy?

Betty: Again, I didn't have opportunity to grieve. During the last three months of Randy's life, I made four trips from Columbia, Tennessee, to Tampa, Florida, to be with him in the hospital. Returning home after that last weekend visit, I received a call on Monday from the hospital advising that Randy was in his final days. I had no way to go back to Florida, so I called my daughter Beth and asked her to check on him. Early Tuesday morning, he seemed to be resting well, so she went to the hotel close to the hospital to get a little rest. The next morning she got the call that Randy had died. That was May 22, 2013.

We had planned to have a memorial service for Randy in October. As a family we were to meet up in Oklahoma City, then travel to my hometown of Rogers, Arkansas, for Randy's service at the cemetery where Duane and my burial sites were. Randy was cremated but we had had a marker for him placed at the foot of our graves.

On route to and in Oklahoma City I began to have mini-strokes. I spent a day in an Oklahoma City hospital. The doctor there had advised that they bring me back to Columbia to be under my doctor's care. So we cancelled the memorial service for Randy and drove to Columbia where they checked me into the hospital at 11:30 p.m. I never got to go back home to Rogers, Arkansas, after that.

———— ✾ ————

Brenda: In what way is it different losing a son and losing a husband?

Betty: I always expected that I would outlive Duane, as women generally outlive men, but Duane's death was sooner than I expected. I did not grieve for Randy as a parent normally grieves for a child, for he had suffered so long, and I knew he was whole again.

———— ✾ ————

Brenda: You reached the time in your life when you had to transition into an assisted living facility. In retrospect, what would have been most helpful to you during that process?

Betty: It would have been better if I could have moved myself, or at least had a say in what to bring to the assisted living. After I was admitted to the nursing home, Rachel and Beth could spend only a few days before they had to go home. They did a good job of equipping my apartment, but no one can make those personal decisions for someone else: books, clothes, and dishes, for example. The apartment is lovely, but I miss lots of my "favorite things."

———— ❀ ————

Brenda: What ministries has the Lord given you with your physical limitations while living in an assisted living facility?

Betty: I feel I have very little to offer now. I have given away several copies of the book, *Muscle and a Shovel.* But the setting here is not conducive to do follow-up as needed. I have made diapers for babies in Third World countries. I try to keep a pleasant attitude toward everyone I encounter. I am trying to do some writing.

———— ❀ ————

Brenda: What are your thoughts as you await your final "homecoming" with the Lord?

Betty: "Lord, take me quickly!"

It's Your Turn

1. What "baton" would you like to pass on to those you leave behind?

2. Regarding marriage: Share a difficult part of your life and how God gave you the victory. What is the best advice you personally would like to share with wives? How could you encourage a preacher's wife? What Scripture is the most helpful to you in your marriage?

3. Regarding motherhood: What one word would you use to describe the mother God wants you to be? Name a Bible character that lives up to that word.

4. Why is grief personal? Why should we let each person grieve in her own way? What did you find most helpful when you grieved the loss of a loved one?

Brenda is the wife of Jack Birckholtz. They have served the churches in New England for forty years. She has taught children's and ladies' Bible classes and speaks at ladies' events. Brenda values her experiences in short-term mission campaigns in Africa, Eastern and Western Europe, Russia, Albania, Canada, and the United States. Her favorite activity is having small groups of ladies in her home for coffee, asking them to bring a favorite scripture to share as they get to know each other as sisters and future friends. She and Jack have three grown children and three grand-children.

Chapter 2

Mentor Me, I Need Someone to Listen

Brenda Birckholtz

*Everyone must be quick to hear, slow
to speak, and slow to anger.*

—— **James 1:19** ——

Listen First

The guiding instruction I received before writing my chapters for this book was,
"If you have the opportunity to sit down with a young woman, or a woman of
any age, what will you say?"

First, I would listen to what she had to say about herself—her past, her
present, and her future aspirations. I would try to listen perceptively to see if
all she wanted was a listening ear. If she wanted me to respond to that which
was shared, hopefully I would respond with sensitivity. If she were to ask me
what the greatest life lessons I've learned over the years, I would share the following ideas: Be your own "pacemaker." And nourish your relationship with
God and others.

*Wisdom is the reward you get for a lifetime of
listening when you would rather have talked.*

—— **Mark Twain** ——

Be Your Own "Pacemaker"

Don't let somebody else set your pace. You and God set it; that will bring you peace. Don't waste your time leading someone else's life. An author whose name I cannot recall said, "Look at your life as a beautiful ongoing painting, and invite God in to be your Michelangelo who will deepen some colors, lighten others, and put shadows and touches where He thinks best." Guard your time well. It is a most precious commodity.

Nourish Your Relationship with God

Nourish is a word to emphasize. Nourish your relationship with God first of all. Someone once said, "A well-fed soul feeds others, bears much fruit, and always has leftovers." I wonder if that is what Jesus meant when He told us, "He who abides in Me and I in him, he bears much fruit" (John 15:5 NKJV). Consider these suggestions for nourishing your relationship with God.

- Daily, even several times a day, "come into His presence with thanksgiving."

- Open up His letters to you (His Word) and drink them in with a thirsty heart, as Paul encourages us to do. "Let the word of Christ richly dwell within you" (Colossians 3:16).

- Humbly submit to all His Word says and be honest with it. With humility comes the promise of exaltation, "Therefore, humble yourselves under the mighty hand of God, that He may exalt you at the proper time" (1 Peter 5:6).

- Let His communication to you excite you, challenge you, and convict you. Growth, challenge, and fulfillment will follow. Talk to Him as your best friend throughout the day. "Thus the Lord used to speak to Moses face to face just as a man speaks to his friend" (Exodus 33:11). Don't we want what Moses had?

- Wait for responses from God through His Word, through others, and through the ordinary circumstances of life. He is always eager to commune with you as best friends do. We have a God who has our back. When the Israelites were preparing to leave captivity and come back to the land of Israel, God assured them, "But you will not go out in haste, nor will you go as fugitives; for the Lord will go before you, and the God of Israel will be your rear guard" (Isaiah 52:12).

- Our caring God has us covered in front and behind. Thank you, God! Because of God's care, we don't have to be frantic or stressed, going out "in haste," or be as those who are running away from someone or some-place—fugitives. We are under His devoted care a hundred percent of the time. Is that not genuine security!

Nourish Your Relationships with Others

Pay attention to your husband, if you have one, and your children, if you have any. Pay attention to your immediate family, extended family, church family, friends, co-workers, acquaintances, and other relationships. Each person has "good news" waiting to be discovered. We must dig a little harder to find it in some people more than others. Each person is a wonderful, mysterious puzzle with many fascinating pieces. How exciting it is to come to know each piece of the puzzle and be amazed at how God is working to make it all fit together. He is doing that for us also. Don't we all hope that those who approach us are looking for some "good news" and "fascinating pieces" in us? To illustrate this idea, please ponder the following scriptures:

- Jeremiah 1:5: "Before I formed you in the womb I knew you, and before you were born I consecrated you." God did know you and consecrated you—set you apart—for His purposes before you were born.

- Jeremiah 29:11: "'For I know the plans I have for you,' declares the Lord, 'plans for welfare and not for calamity to give you a future and a hope.'" Does God have plans for you? Yes, big plans to give you a future and a hope!

- Ephesians 2:10: "For we are His workmanship, created in Christ Jesus for good works, which God prepared beforehand so that we would walk in them." Did God plan specific works for you before the world even began? Yes! *You* are that important to Him.

> *Listen to God with a broken heart. He is not only the doctor who mends it, but the father who wipes away the tears.*
>
> —— Criss Jami ——

The Transformation Process

If you are reading this chapter and looking back at all the "I've blown it" moments in your life, please consider the following: God has taken each "blown it" moment and fashioned it into a beautiful tapestry for His glory, your growth, and a blessing to others. What we perceived as "blown it" moments or years, Christ uses to conform us into His image. Don't let Satan's negative self-talk occlude God's beautiful handiwork. Please give your God an opportunity to shape you into Christlikeness. There are no wasted moments with God! As amazing as it may seem, He is transforming us "from glory to glory" (2 Corinthians 3:18) with each passing day.

"Be Careful How You Listen"—Jesus Christ

Jesus was the greatest listener of all time. Lepers came to Him and He listened (Luke 17:11–19). The blind came to Him and He listened (John 9:1–41). One of the most reciprocal conversations in the Bible is recorded in John 4:4–26 where Jesus listens to the immoral Samaritan woman. The outcome—she came to believe He was the Messiah and helped evangelize her community, Sychar. When we meet Jesus, the only way to go is up. And oh how high He can take us!

There are no wasted moments with God!

Why do I want someone to listen to me? Why do I want someone to mentor me through listening? Well, I have feelings, thoughts, aspirations, disappointments, shocks, and confusion that need to be shared with another caring person. I need a listening ear to help me heal from my disappointments

22

and brokenness. How about you? Also, I have joys, hopes, dreams, aspirations, and plans that I want to share with another caring person. How about you? When someone sincerely listens to me it's like a healing balm, the much-needed medicine I need to restore my soul and deepen my relationship with God. Don't we all have a thirst for the above? Let us share our listening ears with others, and in so doing bring the love of God closer to them.

You're short on ears and long on mouth.

—— John Wayne ——

The Way to the Heart

How can we use listening as a nourishing tool? Start by developing the art of listening. James gives us a helpful passage when he writes, "Be quick to hear [listen], slow to speak, and slow to anger" (James 1:19). The book of wisdom tells us, "If one gives an answer before he hears [listens], it is his folly and shame" (Proverbs 18:13 ESV). And Voltaire is often quoted: "The ear is the avenue to the heart."

If we want to have meaningful friendships, we must become good listeners. That is more easily said than done. Listening takes constant practice and self-control. John Drakeford's book *The Awesome Power of the Listening Ear* is a great help. So is Alan McGinnis's book, *The Friendship Factor.* Chapter 10, "How to Improve Your Conversational Skills," is especially helpful, relating how the author's history teacher shared this incredible bit of wisdom: *The secret of being interesting is being interested.*

The quieter you become the more you hear.

—— Anonymous ——

Use Your Listening Talent

In my early years of elementary school, I perspired and stammered when I spoke, yet I was thirsty for someone to listen to the ideas swirling around in my head. In high school, a teacher listened to me express some of my deep analyzed thoughts and responded positively. In college, another teacher listened and encouraged me to use my talents to serve others. "Talents—what talents?" I thought.

I began to consider developing a "listening" talent to communicate to others their value, just like I wanted someone to communicate mine to me. Thank You, God, for these listeners who inspired me. We can all turn our pain into a listening talent as we sensitize ourselves to the needs of others. Isn't that what God tells us through Paul?

> Blessed be the God and Father of our Lord Jesus Christ, the Father of mercies and God of all comfort, who comforts us in all our afflictions so that we will be able to comfort those who are in any affliction with the comfort which we ourselves are comforted by God" (2 Corinthians 1:3–4).

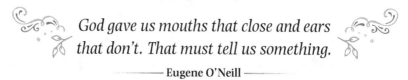

God gave us mouths that close and ears that don't. That must tell us something.

———— Eugene O'Neill ————

Listening Enables Outreach

My sister-in-law Arline is to be commended because of her commitment to my older brother who struggled for years with alcohol and drug abuse, causing considerable pain to the family. Surprisingly she said, "I'm glad we went through those difficult times, because they have brought us to the point we are today." Attending AA and Al-Anon meetings, along with Alateen meetings with their son Brian, taught him valuable lessons to strengthen his life journey."

Additionally Arline said, "We made great friends in the programs which helped us cope with our struggles." Today they have a strong family unit which she credits to having to walk through the stormy challenges of the early years of their marriage. My brother has sponsored hundreds of people in the AA program. My younger brother, Terry, also struggled with alcohol and drug abuse and has mentored many young people as well as his peers. He learned to be a good listener because members of AA and Narcotics Anonymous listened to him. Yes, God comforts us so we can comfort others. As the seasoned members of AA, Al-Anon, and Alateen listened to Barry, Arline, and Brian, they gave them direction and helped them heal. The family in turn reached out and listened to others.

What God Says about Listening

The Bible is not silent about the importance of being attentive.

1. *As He speaks to you in His Word:* "Open my eyes that I may behold wonderful things from Your law" (Psalm 119:18).

2. *As He speaks to you in prayer:* "Pray without ceasing" (1 Thessalonians 5:17).

3. *As He listens to your prayers:* "In the morning, O Lord, you will hear my voice; in the morning I will order my prayer to You and eagerly watch" (Psalm 5:3). Other translations read "I plead my case to you and watch expectantly" or "I lay my requests before you." Note: God wants you to bring your praise and pleadings and needs to Him in the morning, or any other time, and then waiting and watching eagerly or expectantly for His response throughout the day.

4. *As He speaks to you through others:* "Encourage one another day after day" (Hebrews 3:13). The encouragement of others always helps you see God more clearly.

5. *As He provides you with support from others:* "Rejoice with those who rejoice, and weep with those who weep" (Romans 12:15). How we desperately need others to rejoice and weep with us so we can see God in them and they can see God in us.

6. *As He speaks to you through circumstances:* "God causes all things to work together for good" (Romans 8:28). There is no happening in the Christian's life that God isn't working out to His glory and a blessing for all.

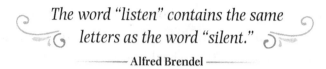

The word "listen" contains the same letters as the word "silent."

—— Alfred Brendel ——

Your Husband Needs Your Listening Ear

No one will listen to your husband like you do. In his place of work and in other situations, he probably has to share time and attention with numerous people. In a very competitive world, your husband probably isn't number one, but he needs to be number one when he walks through the door of your home. With you he needs to know that everything he says is important, even those long boring computer details, or whatever. Ask God to help you be a calm, patient, receptive listener, especially when the topic is not of interest to you. What's even more important is that it is of interest to him. As you nourish your husband by listening, he will be healthy enough to nourish you and others. It's a "win-win situation." By listening we will be living out God's will for us in Ephesians 5:33, that we respect our husbands.

 One of the most sincere forms of respect is actually listening to what another has to say.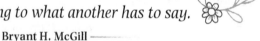

—— Bryant H. McGill ——

Listen to Your Children

We are always telling our children, "Now listen to me! You're not listening!" Let's talk about how important it is to listen to them. They are telling their story, and our response affirms who they are. Children also need to take turns and listen to others. After Christmas break, I would tell our back-to-school children, "All the kids will be excited about their new toys and want to talk about them. But somebody has to listen." If they were fortunate, someone would listen to them.

We emphasized the importance of listening in our family. Although we are a flawed, quite imperfect family, I must say that all three of our children are really good listeners, a trait that has served them well spiritually and socially.

As they reached the teen years, they did not want to be left alone in social settings with a group or an individual they didn't know. They wanted to know what to do in these situations. My answer: "Take time to get to know people." How? By asking them questions about themselves and listening to their answers. After some awkward practices, it was delightful to see all three children, with a degree of comfort, conversing with people of different age groups. It's most gratifying to see our son and his wife teach Brooke, Bailey, and Ben, our grandchildren, to be considerate listeners. Don't you love it when you see the "baton" being passed from one generation to another!

But the art of listening has to be continually practiced. Having grown up in an era where "children are to be seen and not heard," I was left with the impression that what I had to say had no value. Fortunately, some caring teachers along the way and a good counselor communicated to me that I actually had value and something to offer others. I am eternally grateful. If we nourish our children and grandchildren by listening, they will be healthy enough to nourish others. Listen to what is important to them.

Ask God to help you be a calm, patient, receptive listener, especially when the topic is not of interest to you.

Other Family Members

This section is hard for me because I don't come from a close family. My parents are deceased. In the past, five years could easily go by without much communication between me and one of my brothers. So what does one do in these situations? Never miss a birthday: theirs, their wives', or their children's. Either make a call or send a card or text. And always send a Christmas card. Although you can't feed these relationships by listening, you can keep the door open for the future. I have to say in the past few years I've had more frequent conversations with my brothers brought on by one brother's serious health problems. Praise God, we now have meaningful relationships. Maybe my small efforts over the years helped make that transition possible. God takes our mini steps and stretches them into bridges that can build relationships! I'm so thankful.

> *Friends are those rare people who ask how we are, and then wait to hear the answer.*
> — Ed Cunningham

Our Friends

We have some friendships in which we do the majority of listening. This can be difficult but also a blessing. Listening attentively to others blesses their lives and ours. We usually come away with a greater understanding of our friends and their challenges. From these conversations, we come to know how to pray for them and how to lend a helping hand.

Listening Reciprocally

Good listeners need someone who will truly listen to them, I mean truly listen. These are people with whom you have deeper relationships. You share back and forth, and you always make room for each other. It's assumed that confidentiality is a given in listening situations. Take confidentiality seriously. It is the foundation on which relationships are built and deepen. My good friend Mary taught me that confidentiality means that some parts of a conversation need to be kept behind a steel trap door. Our greatest listener is Jesus who encourages us to come to Him, "Come to Me, all who are weary and heavy-laden, and I will give you rest" (Matthew 11:28). Could it be that your listening ear could be the "rest" others desperately need?

Listening in Everyday Events

Quite frequently you have the opportunity to listen to someone in passing, maybe for a few minutes or a few seconds. Just listening to their comments and responding to a sad or enthusiastic tone in their voice can make their day.

You can make someone's day at the 24-hour store, Walmart, on a walk, or any place where a smile, a "hello," or an "I'm sorry" says, "You count."

You and God set your pace and devote yourselves to nourishing others by listening. You will have God's peace and an abundant fulfilled life with many friendships as you listen with your heart to those God places in your path. Your listening can be the path that will lead others to Him. What a talent!

God takes our mini steps and stretches them into bridges that can build relationships!

It's Your Turn

1. Why do you want someone to listen to you?

2. Why do you need to practice listening to others?

3. How do you personally nourish your relationship with God?

4. Share a time when you were "in haste" and feeling like a "fugitive," based on Isaiah 52:12: "But you will not go out in haste, nor will you go out as fugitives; for the Lord will go before you, and the God of Israel will be your rear guard." How did God calm you down and show you He had your back?

5. Consider the effect of these words: "And we know that God causes all things to work together for good for those who love God, to those who are called according to His purpose" (Romans 8:28). How can this verse help you with your perception of and deal with all the "blown it" moments or years in your life?

6. How would it change the world if people truly believed that God "formed you in the womb" and "consecrated you" for His service before you were born (Jeremiah 1:5)?

7. Have you seen God work in your life to "give you a future and a hope" (Jeremiah 29:11)? Share what you have seen. How would a despondent person feel about having "a future and a hope"?

8. How do you feel when you read, "For we are His workmanship, created in Christ Jesus for good works, which God prepared beforehand so that we would walk in them" (Ephesians 2:10)? Read this verse aloud and put your name in the place of "we."

9. Share a time when you were able to comfort others after someone comforted you.

10. Why do you need to listen to God first?

11. Explain how sometimes God is trying to reach you through your friends and through the circumstances of life.

12. How is your husband affected when you listen intently to him for a long time?

13. Suggest ways you can teach your children to become good listeners.

14. What mini steps can you take in difficult relationships to help keep the door open?

15. Why must some of your listening situations be reciprocal for your own spiritual and mental health?

16. Share a time when you made a difference by listening to a stranger.

Listening Extras

1. *Taking Turns.* Partner up with a person, preferably one you don't know very well. Spend five minutes getting to know that person, drawing her out. Do not take back the conversation. It's her time to talk.

Then it is your turn to talk for the next five minutes. At the end of that listening session, ask the group if anyone would like to share something they learned about the person they were listening to.

Here are some conversation starters, but feel free to come up with your own.

a. What is your favorite scripture and why?

b. Share two goals you have set for your life.

c. Who is one of your favorite heroes and why?

d. Describe the person you would like to be.

e. If you could change your life, what would you change?

2. *Self-Evaluation.* Here is a test to give yourself after a conversation.

a. "Did I mostly listen or talk?"

b. "Do I know more about the person than she knows about me?

3. *"Listening" Coffee Event.* Frequently I hold small "coffees" at my home and invite up to ten ladies. I serve light refreshments. Then, having asked the guests to bring a favorite scripture, each begins in turn to tell how her scripture has been helpful in her life. That often leads to lively discussion. Then we eat and continue the "getting to know you" time. As these ladies listen to each other, they build relationships that transfer into making deeper connections within the body of Christ. What a blessing that has been to my life, to see sisters become better friends through listening, coffee, and Scripture.

4. *Special report.* Research or ask a class member to report on Todd Smith's blog, "Ten Ways to Be a Good Listener."[1]

You can make more friends in two months
by becoming interested in other people
than you can in two years by trying to
get other people interested in you.

—— **Dale Carnegie** ——

Laura Dayton has been actively involved in evangelism and serving the Lord's church for over forty years. She is a Bible class teacher for all ages and speaks at ladies' events. Laura is married to Bill Dayton, a gospel preacher. They have served in planting church's and ministry for over thirty years. Laura enjoys singing, playing the piano, reading, and most especially mentoring younger women of all ages in the faith. ✿

Chapter 3

Mentor Me, I'm a First-Generation Christian Woman

by Laura Dayton

She was very excited. Today was the beginning of her new life as a Christian. She was about to attend her first Bible class before Sunday worship. She had never thoroughly read the Bible and was eager to learn all God had to teach her. The study was to be from the book of Jude. As the teacher began, he briefly mentioned that Jude was a study in apologetics. She was a bit confused by this term, so after class went to the teacher and made this comment: "I never dreamed there was a whole book in the Bible that teaches us how to apologize!" The teacher showed much restraint as laughter brewed within. He then patiently explained exactly what the term meant. He was gracious, and she did not feel as ignorant as she might have, but she clearly realized she had a lot to learn.

This humorous true story illustrates the reality that many new Christians are uninformed, even of the basics concerning the Bible.

Who Are These Women and What Do They Need to Know?

The greatest number of new Christians are women, converted from the world and denominational backgrounds. These babes in Christ include single moms, grandmas raising their grandchildren, widows, those divorced and abused, and others with many complicated troubles such as addictions and phobias. As God's dedicated women, we are called to come alongside these precious souls and lend the support and training necessary for them to lead successful and productive lives in Christ. Our involvement is critical to their ability to leave behind the broken world they have been in and embrace a new world that is often foreign and a bit overwhelming. They have lived on the broad way found in Matthew 7:13 which leads to death and is expressed in a self-centered view of everything. Our challenge, if we have the love to accept it, is to demonstrate and teach the narrow way of Matthew 7:14 which leads to life and salvation.

Most of us will never have the time or talent to become professional counselors. Yet God has equipped us to mentor in the spiritual realm. We cannot fix people. We can, however, teach them of the God whose truths can cleanse, restore, and rebuild lives worth living. This is the joy and challenge of mentoring.

> *For we are His workmanship, created in Christ Jesus for good works, which God prepared beforehand that we should walk in them.*
> —Ephesians 2:10

How to Begin

The Scriptures provide three examples of women—all of whom were named in the genealogy of Christ—who were Gentiles, outside of God's covenant and overcome with troublesome circumstances. They are our legacy from God's holy book to help us understand that our heavenly Father is in the redeeming business and will use who He pleases to fulfill His great purposes on earth. These women needed to learn the truth, believe it, and follow the true and living God. They needed to enter into relationships with God's people. As always, God provided.

Today He also provides through His people. We are the hands, arms, voice, feet, face, and heart for Him on earth. We have been given the task of doing His will and sharing His great redeeming love with others. Let's begin. We must accept the work, be equipped, and pray. God will provide the people. He will also provide the truth and the power to share it.

Our first biblical woman is Tamar. Her life record is found in Genesis 38.

A Woman Who Faced Injustice

Tamar first appears in Scripture when Judah selected her to be the wife of his oldest son Er, who was such a wicked man that the Lord killed him (Genesis 38:7). Tamar was a widow and childless and, according to God's law, she was to marry Onan, the next son of Judah. The purpose was to provide an heir for his brother Er. But Onan refused to perform his duty for Tamar. God was displeased and caused his death also.

Then the third son of Judah was enlisted. Shelah was quite young. Tamar was asked to remain single until he became of age to marry. But Judah was clearly concerned that his third son would also die upon marrying Tamar, and ultimately did not keep his word.

Tamar was abandoned and mistreated. When loneliness and bitterness became overwhelming, she took matters into her own hands. She played the harlot, trapped Judah into getting her pregnant, and almost lost her life. Although she bore twin sons, one cannot believe her life was easy. She did not wait on God or consult Him in her time of trial, a terrible mistake repeated by many today.

She Rolled into the Kingdom of God, Literally!

It was late summer. While standing at a corner bus stop, my feet were suddenly attacked by a sharp intrusion. Looking quickly to relieve my discomfort, I saw the end of a skateboard that had stopped a bit past its destination. The rider was a robust young woman in her late teens. She was apologetic and somewhat on edge. Clearly, she was in a hurry to get somewhere. We waited for the bus together.

God's opportunity inspired boldness, and I took a seat next to her on the bus. Our conversation began with simple introductions and observations. Then the real communication began. She, like so many others, is like an open book ready to yield its contents if someone will only take the time to read the pages. After a brief but meaningful exchange, we agreed to meet again. That began a life-long relationship with a remarkable woman who became a Christian and has made a difference for Christ, influencing souls for decades.

Her story was one of a broken home. Her life stung with many injustices all too common in our selfish world. She knew the truth about far too many things that belong to the dark side of life. Yet she was teachable and over time used her "street smarts" to help others find God's way.

> *Come to Me, all you who labor and are heavy laden, and I will give you rest.*
> —Matthew 11:28 NKJV

Mentoring Messages

- *Vengeance belongs to God.* Women need to learn that in spite of the bad things that happen, even to good people, vengeance belongs to God. There is justice in Him (Hebrews 10:30).

- *Seek God's wisdom and instruction.* Before making life-altering decisions, search the Scriptures for counsel. Tamar risked her life to fulfill what she believed was her duty to herself and her future. However, like so many women today, the approach was in seeking solutions without God's approval or guidance. When life seems hopeless and impossible, women need to learn that nothing is impossible for God (Luke 1:37).

- *Trust in God.* So often we limit God, forgetting that He knows best. We fail to trust Him, because often His commands do not make sense to us. We don't know God, because we are too busy asking our peers or consulting Dr. Phil for advice. We trust them more than we trust God (Proverbs 3:5–6; Ephesians 3:20).

- *Bow to the power of forgiveness.* Realize that God's redeeming love is available for all, and we "should not perish" (John 3:16 NKJV). There's room at the cross. So often women have a problem forgiving themselves of sin, so they find it hard to forgive others. Let's not neglect to follow the Lord's example of forgiveness. (See Ephesians 4:32; Matthew 6:5–15; Luke 15:11–32; Colossians 3:13; Luke 17:3.)

A Woman Who Left It All Behind

Rahab was a Gentile citizen of the city of Jericho. Her story is recorded in Joshua 2. She was a prostitute. Rahab knew of the God of Israel and believed in Him and His power from all the stories passed on concerning the victories of Israel. Although a sinful woman, her heart responded to the needs of God's spies sent by Joshua. When she learned that God was going to defeat the evil people of Jericho, Rahab made a deal with the spies. Evidently she was a woman who loved her family and sought to keep them safe. She offered to hide the Israelite spies and set them free over the wall of the city if they would spare her life and those of her family when God granted Joshua and the people victory. Rahab was more than willing to leave her home and possessions behind to follow God's people who provided a refuge and home for her and her family. God further blessed her with a marriage within His people. She is remembered for her faith in Hebrews 11.

> We cannot fix people. We can, however, teach them of the God whose truths can cleanse, restore, and rebuild lives.

A Woman Clothed in Darkness

It was a beautiful sun-filled Sunday morning. The church was gathered and it was time to begin worship when an unfamiliar figure began making her way down the outside border aisle of pews. My back was to her and I was unaware of her presence until I saw a marked shift in the faces of my brethren. An almost audible collective gasp brushed against my ears. Something was happening behind me. I turned and there she was. She was a sight I will never forget.

She was dressed in black from her head to her feet. Her makeup matched the darkness of her attire. She had piercings everywhere. Her eyes moved almost wildly back and forth giving the appearance of sudden terror. Her discomfort was contorted in her expression, and it was apparent that if someone didn't approach her soon, she would bolt to the nearest door, possibly never to return.

Someone needed to approach her with the mindset of a mother welcoming her prodigal daughter home. With only a few moments to greet her, I accompanied my hello with a very gentle touch on the shoulder while beckoning her to join me at my seat.

Her scent was foreign and very heavy. Her constant shifting instructed me to keep my eyes forward and adjust to her need to settle in. Worship ended and thus began the transition into conversation. We went to a private place and talked a long time.

Her story unwrapped like an X-rated novel you would never want to read. She had been sexually abused by both father and uncles, as was her mother. She had run away from home at the age of twelve. Alone and afraid in San Francisco, a seemingly kind couple befriended her. It was a trap. They were heavily involved in the church of Satan. This poor girl was forced into a life of prostitution and pornography. She eventually became a high priestess in this horrid church. She attempted suicide several times. She was almost twenty-two the Sunday I met her. She had decided to make one last effort to escape the agonies of her life.

Within a month, she accepted God's forgiveness, love, and salvation. She obeyed the gospel, and within a few more months departed from her "Jericho" and returned to her mother and a local church awaiting her arrival. We rejoice that God blessed her and us with this wonderful conversion to motivate and inspire others.

Mentoring Messages

- Women need to learn the completeness of God's forgiveness (Psalm 103:1–14).

- Women need to learn the ways of holy women who please God (Proverbs 31).

- Women need to learn about God's unconditional love (Romans 5:5–8)
- Women need to realize that God can further His plan through anyone (Ephesians 2:1–22).

A Portrait of Love, Devotion, and Loyalty

Our final biblical example is Ruth. In the beautiful book that bears her name, this Moabitess outsider demonstrates a heart that was in harmony with the love of God, although she did not yet fully know the extent of God's love. By God's grace she became the daughter-in-law of Naomi, a woman in God's covenant family. Although terrible times befell them, Ruth remained faithful to Naomi and left all family and friends to follow her and her God, the true and living God of Israel. By listening to Naomi's wisdom and attaching herself to her through service and love, Ruth was greatly blessed with a life she had never dreamed possible. She left an example of triumph over misfortune that comes to the person with an obedient and courageous heart.

Entreat me not to leave you, or to turn back from following after you; for wherever you go, I will go; and wherever you lodge, I will lodge; your people shall be my people, and your God, my God.

——— **Ruth 1:16** NKJV ———

A Good-Hearted Woman

From her youth she was a caregiver. Growing up on a farm with many siblings, she found herself happily in the role of nurturer. There was within her a tenderness for those in need and an unquestioned acceptance of her loyalty and duty toward her family. She married young. That love lasted forty-three years, until her husband's parting. Now she was a widow. One thing she had never known was the plan of God's salvation for her life, although she had heard it existed. How could this be in the middle of the Bible Belt? Sadly, her family was much distrusted and disliked for their poverty and waywardness. Although pure in heart, she was shunned by the religious folks at an early age. Despite this rejection, she remained open to the Lord.

God sees the heart. When His people knocked on her door during a campaign, she opened, listened, learned, and obeyed the gospel. To this day, tears well up in her eyes when we sing any song related to the redeeming love of Jesus. Although uneducated by the world's standards, she is wise.

God has blessed her with understanding which is expressed through her talent for writing beautiful poems. She shines like a beacon of God's love as she cares for the elderly in a local nursing home. She, like Ruth, is unwavering in her loyalty and service to God. She has faced illness and loss, but her courage, grounded in Christ, leads her to victory every time.

> *The Lord is near to the brokenhearted and saves those who are crushed in spirit.*
> —Psalm 34:18

Mentoring Messages

- Women need to learn to be wise and understand their worth to God who is not a respecter of persons (Acts 10:34–35).

- Women need to learn God's ways from older women (Titus 2:3–5).

- Women need to trust in God's provision (Matthew 6:26–34).

- Women need to find a way to serve as an expression of love to God and others (Romans 12:3–8; 1 Corinthians 12:4–11).

Summary

Dear sisters, as those under a commission from Christ, we are to go and seek the lost, teaching them to observe all that He has so graciously allowed us to know, we need to ready ourselves for this awesome task. Although the women represented in this chapter by no means reflect the sum total of personalities and backgrounds of women in Scripture or in the world, their example will help our understanding about mentoring first-generation Christian women successfully.

If you are a first-generation Christian, I pray you will find strength and comfort in the knowledge that you are not alone. I also share that heritage with you. God has a plan. His love and salvation are for all! Jesus said:

> Come to Me all you who labor and are heaven laden, and I will give you rest. Take My yoke upon you and learn from Me, for I am gentle and lowly in heart, and you will find rest for your souls. For My yoke is easy and My burden is light (Matthew 11:28–30 NKJV).

If you are attempting to mentor a new Christian sister, begin by lovingly walking by her side. Remember, you cannot fix her life. She needs the truth that can make her free (John 8:32). Some may be suffering from the abuses of others or from the earned miseries of their own choices. Guilt, fear, and anger are the byproducts of sin. Seek God, study, and instruct her in the faith. Live a life worth imitation. Be patient; be a sister. Bring her into your family and help her to feel a part of your life. Be a trusted confidant and friend. Be a servant. Above all, be like Jesus. Then you, along with her, will bear much fruit unto love and good works.

It's Your Turn

1. In your sphere of influence, is there someone who has not obeyed the gospel? If so, begin by praying every day for one week that you will be given an opportunity to have a spiritually focused conversation.

2. Is there a new sister within your congregation who has come from a difficult background? Make an effort to spend time with her, even if it is just for a cup of coffee.

3. Organize a small gathering or Bible study group to include this new sister. Statistics clearly indicate that for new Christians to remain faithful, they need to make a real connection with at least five people.

4. Are you ready to share your faith? Are you prepared to help a new Christian grow? If not, then seek out someone who can give you information to study. Remember, we have been called out for a purpose.

I couldn't even count the number of friends who have said to me, "I wish I had taken the time to be single longer in order to be a more mature person when I married." Use your singleness as a special time in your life to respond to His unique calling. Let the timing be God's as you bring glory to Him each day of your life, serving Him in ways that are especially designed for the gifts He has given only you.

—Brenda Birckholtz

CHAPTER 4

Mentor Me, I'm a
Single
Christian Woman

by Brenda Birckholtz

How is *singleness* defined? An indictment, a punishment, a disease, a destiny, or a discipleship? The impressions of the word are as varied as the person defining it.

God thinks noble things of single people. Jesus, Paul, Jeremiah, and others were single, and God mightily used them. If for whatever reason God is allowing you to be single, use your single calling in a powerful way until God changes your situation. I didn't marry until I was almost thirty-two. A friend of mine didn't marry until she was forty-nine. At her wedding ceremony, after the minister pronounced the couple "man and wife," he said, "Finally!" This is not what a single girl wants to hear!

Having been raised a serious Catholic, I knew enough not to marry until I was sure the marriage would last forever. While dating I could never be sure that the relationship would last forever. At age twenty-five I became a follower of Jesus. I had searched for many years to find the meaning of life. I found the meaning of life in Jesus. Dr. Viktor Frankl, psychoanalyst and author of *Man's Search for Meaning,* survived four Nazi concentration camps including Auschwitz and Dachau. He observed that his fellow prisoners could survive the suffering and degradation if they could find meaning in life, meaning in the suffering. We can survive anything, any suffering, any circumstance when we find the meaning of life, Jesus Christ.

The day after my baptism into Christ I began thinking that shortly God would send me "the one," because now I had seen that He truly was the way, the truth, and the life. However, even though I was committed to Him, God knew that I was not prepared for marriage. What follows is His training program to help me see what "life in the Son" is truly about.

God kept putting me in situations that would teach me that life was not about me. In reality, any relationship does not work out well until you are convinced that "it is more blessed to give than to receive" (Acts 20:35).

I was facing internal struggles almost daily. I wondered why God allowed me to be single for so long.

God placed me in a little vibrant mission congregation in Massachusetts. The minister and his wife, Duane and Betty Bender, along with their co-workers, Reagon and Rachel Wilson, challenged me in ways I had never thought possible. They gave me opportunities to teach children's Bible classes, ladies' Bible classes, and one-on-one evangelistic studies. They also modeled before me the need to visit the lonely and the sick, and to send cards, make calls, take food, and give people rides to church and doctors. Note: A single girl always has room in her car for others, right?

Were all of these challenges pleasant? No. Some were difficult, but it was all part of my training and preparation for the future God had planned for me. He was showing me how to behave in His family of believers, which later translated into knowing how to behave in a "mom, dad, and the kids" family. As this training program was going on, everybody was blessed. God was causing all things to "work together for good" (Romans 8:28). I was blessed because I was taking advantage of "giving" opportunities. The people

I served were blessed. My mentors were blessed because they felt like John did when he wrote, "I have no greater joy than to hear that my children are walking in the truth" (3 John 1:4 ESV).

> *When we cannot stand to be alone, it means we do not properly value the only companion we have from birth to death—ourselves.*
> —Eda LeShan

Internal Struggles

In reality, I was facing internal struggles almost daily. I wondered why God allowed me to be single for so long. Was I unattractive? Was I just too dysfunctional? Was He punishing me for past sin? Did He need single missionaries more than He needed married women to glorify Him?

As I drove to work each day, I told God that I didn't like the single life but that I would try to accept it. Deeper acceptance happened after I heard a lesson by Jim McGuiggan, brotherhood author and speaker, at a lectureship in Troy, Ohio. Challenging us to explore how much we would accept God's will, he proposed the following questions:

- What if it suited God's purposes for you to be in the corner of a hospital room somewhere with an incurable debilitating disease for the rest of your life?
- What if God took away your speech, your sight?
- What if God wanted you to remain childless?
- What if God wanted you to remain single for the rest of your life so that you could glorify Him in ways you couldn't as a married woman?

What? I didn't expect or like that last question, but my heart was pricked. After the lesson, I went into a field alone, and God and I had "the talk." Does God provide open fields for reflection and conversation with Him right outside a lectureship facility? Yes! I cried and told God that I didn't think I could resign myself to eternal singleness and was a little—okay, a lot—upset that He would ask this of me. After a period of time and being nudged by my conscience, I told God, "Okay, if it is Your will for me, I will serve You as a single, I will." Let me add that the human part of me had to renew that contract countless times before I would meet the man I married.

 I'm not single because I don't pray for love. I'm single because I don't play around with love.
—Unknown

Who Will Help Me Get to Heaven?

Of course you want to know how long I had to wait until God sent me the person He wanted me to marry. I waited six years after I became a New Testament Christian, two years after I talked with God in the field and submitted my will to His. In the meantime, He provided opportunities for me to work for Him on short-term mission trips to Africa, Eastern and Western Europe, Canada, and several American cities. He also challenged me to serve Him in a host of other ways. The open doors for service never stopped.

In the fullness of His time, God sent me a kind, gentle, spiritual man. My husband, Jack, was well-worth the wait, because he is truly the spiritual wind beneath my wings.

If and when your time to marry comes, please be very cautious. If that potential husband doesn't have Jesus as the center of his life, marriage is not an option. Do not let anyone toy with your spirituality or even take a micro-particle of it away. As a matter of fact, look for someone who is more spiritually mature than you. Why not upgrade, right? Hey, everybody likes a good deal, especially a spiritual good deal. I knew that I had paid many

> God thinks noble things of single people. Jesus, Paul, Jeremiah, and others were single, and God mightily used them.

prices learning life lessons on the way to the good news of Jesus, and nobody was going to put my salvation in jeopardy. Recently my friend Becky told us what her criteria for choosing a husband was: Who will be the best person to help me get to heaven?

While in a serious relationship with another man, Becky met Todd. She could see that he would be the best man to help her get to heaven. She ended that relationship and married Todd, a very spiritually minded man who is now an elder.

One of my co-authors, Becky Blackmon, recently shared with us a story about her daughter Jennifer's future husband Tim. When Tim asked Becky and her husband Jeff for Jennifer's hand in marriage, Becky and Jeff said, "If you will promise us that you will help Jennifer get to heaven, you can have her hand in marriage." Isn't that impressive? The request by the parents tells me that their daughter's spiritual life was much more important than just having a married life.

> Any relationship does not work out well until you are convinced that "it is more blessed to give than to receive" (Acts 20:35).

> The unmarried woman cares about the things of the Lord, that she may be holy both in body and in spirit. But she who is married cares about the things of the world—how she may please her husband (1 Corinthians 7:34 NKJV).

I couldn't even count the number of friends who have said to me, "I wish I had taken the time to be single longer, in order to be a more mature person when I married." This comment validates the fact that the best road to travel, whether you are single, married, divorced, widowed, or whatever, is the path of service to others. Use your singleness as a special time in your life to respond to His unique calling. Let the timing be God's as you bring glory to Him each day of your life, serving Him in ways that are especially designed for the gifts He has given only you.

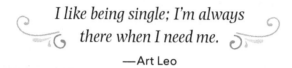

*I like being single; I'm always
there when I need me.*

—Art Leo

What Can We Do for Singles?

1. Be sensitive to their need for "family." Include them in your family activities and holidays.

2. Respectfully challenge them to use their talents in various areas of service.

3. Be especially mindful of them in a group, never neglecting to introduce them to others and include them in conversation.

4. Be considerate of not "highlighting" their singleness. Don't continually try to "fix" their situation.

5. Some people love being single. Leave room for God's loving hand to work.

6. Be respectful of their time. Do not assume they do not have a life. For instance, do not presume they will be your backup babysitter or that they can do last-minute tasks.

What Can Singles Do?

Embrace your singleness as a special calling from the Lord at this stage of life. Understand the honor He has given you by inviting you to walk with Him into the lives of others.

1. Pray for God to show you the many ways He can use you in your present situation.

2. Be aware of your various gifts and how they can bless others.

3. Take the first step in meeting others. So many are in need.

4. Reach out to all ages. They are waiting to be "met."

5. Get on board in a ministry or a volunteer program. Great programs succeed or fail depending on committed participants.

6. Be creative in your serving.

Suggestions for Service

1. *Invite families, a group of people, or another single to join you for a meal or a snack after church or at some other convenient time.* People love to be invited. These meetings give others an opportunity to get to know you and you them. Both as a single and as a married person, I enjoyed the simplicity of Burger King, McDonald's, and Panera for my restaurant ministry. For the most part, I never felt the need to pay for these outings. People are fine with that.

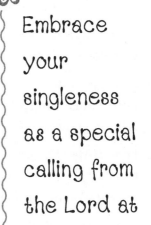

Embrace your singleness as a special calling from the Lord at this stage of life.

2. *Babysit someone else's children.* Even two or three hours frees a busy mother to visit someone or run errands.

3. *Visit people in hospitals, nursing homes, or those who are homebound.* Note: People who need long-term care are easily forgotten. Also, long-term caregivers are often in need.

4. *Tutor free of charge or mentor children who are in need.* Just an hour here or there could make a big difference in a young person's life.

5. *Host a devotional at your house with light refreshments to follow.* "Light refreshments" means cheese and crackers, fruit, and dessert (store-bought is fine), or any combination of your choosing. It's important to keep everything "light," which means simple!

6. *Host a game night at your house.*

7. *Plan a mystery dinner or progressive dinner.* During progressive dinners guests travel to three different households in the course of an evening. The first

stop is for appetizers, the second, the main meal, and the third, dessert. Again, make the menu simple.

8. *Plan an interest-based outing.* Bowling, skiing, ice skating, sports events, or a movie. Bring people back to your house for a devotional and snacks.

9. *Promote a restaurant-devo night.* Plan to go to a restaurant with the express purpose of having a devotional during the meal or after you eat. The goal is to bring the group back to God who is the sustainer of all relationships.

10. *Form a "Meet Up" group.* Online there is a "Meet Up" group where people get together just to read the Bible. Why not start your own Scripture-reading "Meet Up" group at a place of your choosing?

11. *Start a book club.* Choose a book of a spiritual nature and grow closer to each other as you discuss and share ideas about the book.

I haven't even scratched the surface of the number of ways singles can plan get-togethers that bring them closer to the Lord and to each other. That's up to you, singles. Hey, think of publishing your own book or booklet that sets forth the myriad of ways singles can meet the needs of other singles! The above suggestions provide opportunities for you to mentor each other. As always, make God the center.

It's Your Turn

1. Why must we have absolute confidence in God's timing as we wait and hope He will send us "the one"?

2. What are your thoughts on the following: Could it be that we are not ready for marriage and that we need more training and preparation before it happens?

3. Are there areas in your life in which you feel you need more preparation for marriage? Feel free to share but feel free not to share and use this time for personal reflection.

4. Share some activities that can be accomplished as a single person but cannot be accomplished as a married person.

5. Share some great positives about the single life.

6. Paul writes, "Now to Him who is able to do far more abundantly beyond all that we ask or think, according to the power that works within us . . ." (Ephesians 3:20). Is God working "exceeding, abundantly beyond all that we ask or think through the power that works in us" (NKJV), no matter what our marital status is?

7. Describe some ways He's working in your life right now.

8. What does the following quote mean to you? "The time you are in is God's gift to you."

arty has been a Christian since 1974. She and her husband Frank, a gospel preacher, have served in the capital region of Upstate New York for forty-five years. She taught second grade in the public-school system in their hometown of Clifton Park, retiring in 2007. She has taught all ages of children and women in Bible classes, spoken at ladies' retreats, and conducted teachers' workshops in the Northeast. Her interests include downhill skiing in the scenic Adirondack Mountains and gardening. One of her favorite experiences has been conducting and reading to children in story-time programs. Frank and Marty have three grown children and seven grandchildren.

Chapter 5

Mentor Me, I'm Teaching My Child about God

by Martha Coletta

The Love Tap

Duane and Betty Bender invited our family to dinner one Sunday after worship. Frank and I, along with our four-year-old son John, looked forward to this intimate fellowship with friends. Duane was serving as an elder at Clifton Park. I taught with Betty in the wives' program at the Northeast School of Biblical Studies. Frank served as dean of students, as well as being an instructor for the men studying to become preachers. It was nice to be on the receiving end of a dinner invitation, and we looked forward to having a wholesome Sunday afternoon visit.

Dinner met all of our expectations, as Betty served a lovely casserole and dessert. We were sharing funny family stories and laughing together when, during a lull in the conversation Duane said, "There's something that Betty and I would like to discuss with you." Within a heartbeat, things turned serious.

Frank and I had been Christians for twelve years. We considered ourselves successful parents, having witnessed our two daughters putting on Christ several years before. They were then serving at Camp Hunt as junior counselors. Our surprise son, John, at four, was in some ways being raised as an only child. His two siblings were ten and eleven years older.

"We've noticed some things that we'd like to bring to your attention about what you're doing with John," began Papa Duane. "Betty and I have observed many times that John doesn't respond to you when you ask him to do something. He just continues doing what he wants until you move to physically make him obey."

"Hmmm," said Frank, looking down at nothing.

Betty continued, "Even today at the table you asked John several times to sit up and stop kicking under the table. He just kept on, as if you didn't say anything. And then, he got up from the table without permission and left to go play with his toys in the living room."

Frank and I basically listened to their advice, well-intended but difficult to hear, even though I had to admit it was true—grudgingly. We responded in what must have been appropriate ways, because we stayed for a while longer. In a way as timely as possible, we thanked them for their concern and sharing with us and prepared to go home. We had a lot to think about.

Frank firmly told John to pick up his toys; he did. We hugged our elder and his wife, said our *thank yous* and *goodbyes*, and drove off to our home.

Hurt Feelings

Silence. We were stunned. Truthfully, our pride was damaged. Many feelings surfaced.

Arrival at home brought some equilibrium and, I'm sure, an answer to prayer. Telling the story from years later, I have no doubt that Duane and Betty were in active prayer as we left.

Our first comments to each other affirmed that we both felt hurt in hearing that our parenting skills were lacking. And then, amazingly, Frank said, "They're right. We have been slacking with John. We never would have let Michelle or Christine do what he was allowed to do at the table."

Thank You, God, for Frank. He strives to live what he teaches from the Scriptures. His leadership in our family is honest and always striving to do what is right.

We talked about how courageous and loving it was for Duane and Betty to approach such a delicate subject with us. They trusted that we would listen, reflect, and follow this instruction: "But speaking the truth in love, we are to grow up in all aspects into Him who is the head, even Christ" (Ephesians 4:15).

Here's a thought: How sad when young, and even older parents, because of pride and arrogance, cannot take counsel from older wiser Christians who are speaking truth in love. It takes trust and courage to do so; it takes humility to listen and reflect.

Discipline in Action

We put band aids on our wounded pride, acknowledged our lazy parenting that had allowed John to be disobedient, and began to plan ways to guide him in obedience and responsibility. We even enrolled in a parenting course offered by a teacher we knew in the community. We saw and celebrated the small but significant changes that happened because of more effective parenting, not only in John but in our own approach to parenting.

The Scriptures are clear about our responsibility as parents.

> Children, obey your parents in the Lord, for this is right. "Honor your father and mother," which is the first commandment with promise: "that it may be well with you and you may live long on the earth." And you, fathers, do not provoke your children to wrath, but bring them up in the training and admonition of the Lord (Ephesians 6:1–4 NKJV).

We know how important it is for these tender souls to learn obedience to us, their parents, if they are ever going to respond in obedience to God. The responsibility to train them up to know God is awesome and humbling.

I am ever grateful for two loving people who took the time to sit with us and talk. They cared enough to risk our relationship to help us see more clearly what was really happening with our son. That talk has gone many, many miles, more than they ever imagined.

It has also provided a model for us in our older years, as we see parenting going on about us, especially with our own grandchildren. How difficult it is to confront friends, in as loving a way as possible, when you see something that needs correction. It makes me appreciate even more how much Duane and Betty loved us and must have prayed for wisdom and boldness as they approached us.

Love Your Children

Older women are to train the younger women to love their children.

> Older women, likewise are to be reverent in their behavior, not malicious gossips nor enslaved to much wine, teaching what is good, so that they may encourage the young women to love their husbands, to love their children, to be sensible, pure, workers at home, kind, being subject to their own husbands, that the word of God will not be dishonored (Titus 2:3–5).

Note the observations of this scholar.

> A study of the context of Titus 2:3–5 guides us to understand that Titus had a tough assignment from the apostle Paul, who had been there to help establish God's church on Crete, but who also left Titus to continue the maturing process. The Cretans are characterized in chapter 1 as "liars, evil beasts, lazy gluttons." Paul is quoting a sixth century BC Cretan philosopher, Epimenides, who was using the literary technique of a hyperbole (exaggeration) in describing all Cretans. The point made by Paul was, while not every Cretan was lazy and a liar, the society there as a whole was characterized as such. Further, Cretans were responding to the gospel message, coming out from a pagan background.[1]

In this letter to Titus, Paul wastes no time in stating his purpose: Contend for the faith! Get elders appointed—godly men qualified to guide, to protect, to admonish, and even to refute error. Help these young Christians hold the course.

Paul had great trust that Titus would follow through, even to teaching the older and more mature women to train young mothers who had put on Christ, but perhaps needed strong Christian models to help them cement godly principles in their lives and in the lives of their children. Their assignment: Teach what is good! Specifically, harmonizing with the theme of this chapter—ways to love their children, training them in everyday goodness. This charge is still valid for today.

Again I say, I will ever be thankful for two older Christians who took the time to share with us, even though it meant risking a relationship. We were blind to what was happening and they helped us to see.

A Survey with Young Mothers

When considering the "Titus 2 charge" in my twenty-first century life, I surveyed several young mothers with this question: "What are your thoughts about older women mentoring younger women, specifically as it relates to raising their children?"

The answers sounded very much the same and went something like this:

- There should first be an established relationship based on love and trust.
- The older woman should ask permission before giving advice.

I consider these comments to be thoughtful, ones that certainly make sense in any kind of mentoring venue, especially with childrearing. This is a very sensitive area, but one in which mentoring, whether formal or informal, is desperately needed. It doesn't take much investigation today to find that our children are growing up in a society where disrespect has reached epidemic proportions. The Epimenides hyperbole could easily relate to today with slight tweaking. Our children will hopefully mature to be like Christ.

> For those whom He foreknew, He also predestined to become conformed to the image of His Son, that He would be the firstborn among many brethren (Romans 8:29).

But they need strong Christian parents who put God first in their lives and the home, and then train those precious souls to know what is good.

If love and trust are already established through normal extended family activities, then the stage has been set for effective mentoring, whether formal or impromptu. Even under these conditions, it is not often easy to mentor as Duane and Betty did with us. My husband and I have learned as the older and—"ahem"—wiser ones to adhere to the following principles.

- Listen first.
- Validate comments by repeating back what you've heard.
- Ask for time to think and pray about the issue.
- Give advice only if it is solicited or if you have permission.
- Be available for feedback and further reflection.

A Good Use of Our Media

Talking with parents about what we see going on with their children is tricky business. We have concerns, yes, and we understand that we can give advice if it is solicited. Most times it is not. We find ourselves making comments to each other about the behaviors we've witnessed but do not feel comfortable addressing them to the parents. Relationships among brethren today are often limited by "Hi" and "How's it going?" with not much getting below the surface. Mentoring takes time, sometimes sharing things that are not comfortable to say, and prayerfully being sensitive as well as creative.

There is a great television series called *Supernanny*. Jo Frost is the mentor/teacher who is invited into homes where families are in chaos. The children are usually acting way out of control, often in unsafe situations and clueless about respectful behavior. Truly this is not far from the norm in some families today. Parents are ineffective in their techniques to discipline and direct the children. No one is happy.

After being allowed to observe for a day, Jo talks with the parents, stating the facts of what she has seen. Strategies are introduced, modeled by Jo, and then practiced by the parents. New techniques for addressing inappropriate behavior actually take less energy on the part of parents and empower their children to make right choices. Time is given for reflection. The episodes always end happily with parents and children hugging Jo as she leaves to help another family. A little bit of Hollywood going on here, but with some valid information for parents and older mentors to thoughtfully weigh.

My husband and I have used parts of these episodes in parenting classes we have offered during Bible study times. We have learned that when folks are not confronted directly, they have less trouble applying the teaching to their own situations and needs. Doors open easier to share other concerns. This approach encourages discussion. Later reports from parents validated that Jo's strategies worked and that they loved the difference! Besides Jo's input, we have been able to supplement with biblical teaching that cements the concepts for parents. In other words, again teaching what is good. Please note that we did check with copyright laws before showing these excerpts to our audiences.[2]

> *The Bible class teacher explained to the preschoolers,*
> *"God makes trees and water and apples and cherries.*
> *God makes everything." Immediately one little*
> *boy complained, "God doesn't make my bed!"*[3]

Wake Up, Sweet Child

My special passion is in helping young parents recognize and cherish their God-given responsibility to teach their children about our Lord and help them grow in their own faith. I love it when I find young parents who respond positively and act on what they know to be true.

> He established a testimony in Jacob and appointed a law in Israel, which he commanded our fathers to teach to their children, that the next generation might know them, the children yet unborn, and arise and tell them to their children, so that they should set their hope in God and not forget the works of God, but keep his commandments (Psalm 78:5–7 ESV).

This psalm urges parents to teach their children about God, that the generations to follow might know of Him and have their confidence in Him. It harmonizes with Deuteronomy 6:4–9, a timeless guidepost for Dad and Mom.

Sarah was an older first-time mother. She and her husband were young Christians who did not have family living nearby. They had adopted little Becky as a newborn. Nora, an older woman in the church, felt honored to be considered Becky's surrogate grandmother. It was her joy to watch this sweet baby grow and discover the world around her. When the time came for little Becky to begin to attend cradle role, Nora was sad to realize that Becky was always absent. How she had looked forward to being her first Bible class teacher. It was natural for Nora to speak to Sarah about this. Perhaps others can relate to Sarah's response.

"Well, you see, Nora, Becky sleeps in and doesn't wake up in time for us to get her ready for Bible class."

Nora digested this, prayed silently for wisdom, and then replied with a little giggle, "So here's what you could do. Tip toe into her room, singing a little wake up song, tickle her on her shoulder and say, 'Wake up, Becky! Time for Bible class.'"

Sarah looked at Nora and then broke into a huge giggle of her own. She understood at that moment how silly it sounded to have a one-year-old set the pace for the whole family attending Bible class. The next Sunday Becky took her place at the cradle role table and delighted her mother, who stayed to observe.

Within six months Sarah was able to take Nora's chair and teach her daughter the songs and actions she had seen so often. A memorable scene commenced: mother teaching daughter about God.

Grab That Baton and Run with It!

It is of great concern to me when I see young parents today passing the baton of teaching their children off to Granny or Grandpa or to the Bible class teacher. They are too busy, or they often hide behind the excuse that it is not their talent. Hogwash! Teaching our own children does not take a special gift from Christ. It is a responsibility parents have accepted as part of raising a child. And further, I am not advocating that every parent needs to be a Bible class teacher; however, it is God's command that parents teach their children about their Creator and His will for them. Moses gave the original teaching instructions for the following settings: "When you sit in your house and when you walk by the way and when you lie down and when you rise up" (Deuteronomy 6:7).

This is where mentoring as a seasoned Bible class teacher can be of value. I delight in using my abilities as a teacher of children, sharing techniques and ideas that have been developed through the years. My goal is for parents to see different ways they can have fun teaching and influencing their children about God at home. An added bonus is when a parent steps into the role of Bible class teacher because of things he or she has learned and is willing to do.

A setting in which I have had opportunity to train is the Bible classroom. My focus in recent years has been with the younger children, from nursery through four- and five-year-olds. It is especially rewarding to have parents accept my invitation to stay and learn how to share God's Word with their little ones. And parents do seem to enjoy watching their own children interact.

Our twos and threes classroom is large enough to have stations, different areas in the room where aspects of the theme can be taught. The theme is in place for the whole quarter, so children hear the stories many times. We have found this to be a very effective way to cement Bible stories for young children, as well as to provide a venue for parents to observe and learn. Planning is minimal after the room is set up. One grandmother shared with me that her two-and-a-half-year-old grandson couldn't wait for Bible class.

> Mentoring takes time, sometimes sharing things that are not comfortable to say, and prayerfully being sensitive as well as creative.

"Oh, you like Bible class?" asked Granny.

"No, I love Bible class," replied the articulate youngster. How wonderful when the parents' curiosity brought them to the classroom to stay and see what was happening.

Encouraging parents of young children to come and observe is a very effective way to show how you can teach simple Bible concepts, even to babies. And where else should it all start? I think I recall reading that Grandmother Lois and Mother Eunice had a sincere faith which was transferred to Timothy.

> For I am mindful of the sincere faith within you, which first dwelt in your grandmother Lois and your mother Eunice, and I am sure that it is in you as well (2 Timothy 1:5).

Obviously they lived their faith and began teaching their faith to Timothy in his young years, perhaps even before he could talk. How beautiful when among a child's first words one might hear "Jesus" or "Bible." A great way to instill a child's concept of God is through repetition of singing songs, such as "Jesus, Name above All Names" and "The Love of God."

Pass the Baton

I had the pleasure of watching our one-year-old grandson while his mother continued, reluctantly, with her teaching career for one final year. Each day began with breakfast in the high chair, followed by a Bible story and songs, using various toys and objects that he could manipulate.

It was no surprise to me that when she later elected to become a stay-at-home mother, she used many of the same toys to continue the teaching in her own home.

This segued to formal Bible class teaching as she stepped up to teach her six-month-old second child in the nursery class. On her first Sunday, I peeked in before class, a friendly Nana visit. I could tell she was agitated as she monitored her young son, already in the chair insert of the table, playing with a large block puzzle.

She began to weep quietly. I listened to her concerns and learned that she was anxious about her abilities to teach the lesson when the other babies arrived. The dynamics of a cradle roll class can be daunting, but I knew she was up for it. She had monitored while I taught her first little boy for almost a year. That's mentoring, by the way. She knew her stuff. She was ready.

I validated her feelings and asked her if we could pray together right there. She nodded and I asked God to bless her with strength, good memory, and most of all joy as she taught these little ones. Since then she has not stopped teaching, except to have another baby—her third little boy.

An epilogue to this story is that she has since mentored other young mothers in how to teach their babies in the cradle roll class. A perfect passing of the baton.

Good Night, Sleep Tight!

Monica was grandmother to three lovely little girls. She looked forward to those times when she could be with them and with her beautiful daughter-in-law. One evening she was at their home, helping to put the two older girls to bed. Daddy was still at work. And Mother was in an adjoining room nursing her youngest. Monica had both little ones on the large bed, reading them favorite bedtime stories. As the last page was turned, she suggested that they sing a few Bible songs about Jesus. The girls loved the one about Peter, James, and John in a fishing boat. Three-year-old Sarah always liked to walk Jesus along her arm. They finished with "The Wise Man/Foolish Man" song, building his house on the rock. Then six-year-old Susan asked, "Granny, why did he build his house on a rock?"

What a simple opportunity to teach! Without getting overly involved, Granny Monica explained that the song was about choosing Jesus, and the rock in the song was really Jesus and His teachings. She sang the rest of the verses for them, using the appropriate hand motions to go along with the words. That song is now theirs, as well as their mother's, who just might have been listening from the other room. She experienced an impromptu training lesson on how to teach as you go, plus how bedtime can be an opportunity to teach about God. Monica didn't have to say another word.

There's no doubt that parents are tired at the end of the day and look to the quiet of the evening to soothe and pamper themselves. How good it is to recognize these moments as priceless times to share God's love and wonder. It doesn't have to take long. Is there any better way to send little minds off to sleep?

Epilogue: Younger to Older—How It Continues

The new house was still dark in the early hours of the morning. Five-year-old Jackson had awakened in his own darkened room. The hall light cast shadows on the wall as an open window allowed curtains to flow with the wind. It frightened Jackson to the point of arising from bed and going into his parents' bedroom.

"Daddy," whimpered the little boy. "Where's Mommy? I need her."

Still exhausted from a long day at work and needing these quiet hours to sleep, Daddy rolled over and told Jackson to go back to bed.

"But Daddy, where's Mommy?"

"She's downstairs, Jack, with your baby brother. She's feeding him downstairs."

"Can you go with me so I can see her?"

"No, Jack. You can go by yourself. I'm going back to sleep." And he rolled over.

The little boy knew Daddy meant business. He left the bedroom, venturing toward the stairs.

Realizing his son was gone, Daddy listened for footsteps. And then he heard, "God cares for me, God cares for me, God cares for me; He's so good to me." The precious voice of a young child rang out as he descended those dark stairs in search of his mother.

The following Sunday our son John shared a brief talk at worship. What do you suppose he opened with? A story about his little boy in the middle of the night. Jack reminding Daddy to have faith that God will take care of us.

So often modern mentoring happens in the small opportunities that present themselves "as you go"—like the little songs that a grandmother might sing to her son and then to her grandson. Treasured moments are found in small things, too. Like a child descending the dark stairs and calming himself with that same song about God's love.

While the father was indeed reflecting on the transference of his faith to his young son, grandmother was thinking of her own little boy who, many years before, had been the topic for a while at a Sunday afternoon dinner.

For my husband and me it all began with a loving couple who mentored us in seeing ways we could improve our parenting skills with our son. That same son grew to become a father, a father who heard his son remind him in song that God will take care of us. He loves us so.

It's Your Turn

1. How do you see Deuteronomy 6 active in your home?

2. What is one of your favorite Bible stories that you heard as a child? How could you present it to your child?

3. What children's books have you used that lend themselves to biblical teachings?

4. Read Psalm 78:5–7. Why are these verses still important for us today?

5. Cite a memory verse that you would like your child to learn. How could you help him/her learn it?

6. What Christian songs do you and your family sing together?

7. Tell of a teachable moment with your child when you were able to share God's Word.

8. If you can, share a behavior issue that is of concern to you as a parent. Listen for godly advice from the older women who are sharing this study with you.

It's challenging for family members to even take time to look into one another's eyes and communicate. Instead, Dad or Mom issues a steady flow of directives. They hustle in the morning when everyone, including baby, is leaving home. All family members are doing their own thing during the busiest, most productive part of the day, returning by late afternoon exhausted, but needing to plow through a quick dinner, often not together, so someone can be at soccer, baseball, or tennis practice. TV tells a story to little Johnny, and baby Sarah is entertained by the automatic swing before bath and sleep. Next morning it happens all over again as the alarm announces the start of a new day. Where is the quality time to listen, to respond, and to share insights into God's Word?

—Martha Coletta

66

Chapter 6

Mentor Me, I'm a Busy Parent

by Martha Coletta

I'm Just Like You, Dad

In 1974 Harry Chapin introduced a song, "Cat's in the Cradle." It became an instant hit and was broadcast many times each day on the radio. The message of the song was simple: Dad, Mom, you're the model for your children. Spend quality time with them now. Don't be like the parent of the song, where "we'll get together then" evolved into "never." The son grew up just like Dad, not having time to spend with him. Too busy! He learned well.

If I had only one message to pass along to parents with young children, it would be this one: You are the most influential person in your child's world now. That will change over time. Therefore, spend quality time with your child now. I'm not talking about attending sporting events, school, and church functions, or activities where you're the spectator and your child performs. Those are all good and should be done, but they must not take the place of those jewels of time when it's one-on-one. These are the nuggets of time that do not have to be lengthy. The debate of "quality versus quantity" time is waged often in parenting books. But don't we all know that without a sufficient quantity of time, we might miss the quality time? These are slots of time to listen, to respond, to laugh together, to build memories, to influence, to share what we hold dear in life—our walk with God. As Christian parents, we've had that directive all along in the following verses of Deuteronomy.

Now this is the commandment, the statutes and the judgments which the Lord your God has commanded me to teach you, that you might do them in the land where you are going over to possess it, so that you and your son and your grandson might fear the Lord your God, to keep all His statutes and His commandments which I command you, all the days of your life, and that your days may be prolonged . . . you should listen and be careful to do it, that it may be well with you and that you may multiply greatly, just as the Lord, the God of your fathers, has promised you . . . You shall love the Lord your God with all your heart and with all your soul and with all your might. These words, which I am commanding you today, shall be on your heart. You shall teach them diligently to your sons and shall talk of them when you sit in your house and when you walk by the way and when you lie down and when you rise up. You shall bind them as a sign on your hand and they shall be as frontals on your forehead. You shall write them on the doorposts of your house and on your gates (Deuteronomy 6:1–9).

In the context, God was telling Moses that the strength of the Israel nation rested in the health of the family. The key to that health was in keeping God and His commands at the center of the family. There were many challenges yet before them, and they needed to know where their trust, faith, and hope were anchored.

This continues to apply to Christian parents today. Our day-in-day-out lives must reflect an obedient faithful walk with God. His commands abide in our hearts first. He is our priority. Our lives, especially before our children and their children, need to reflect this. No hypocrisy, no masks.

As our children see how we walk in this world, they will have healthy models to follow. They learn to practice God's way along with us. And we do know that the challenges to live godly in this world are daunting. Sin in all of its many varieties flows easily through our society. It is a comfortable member in many homes. May we take sin seriously with awareness of the urgency of living and teaching God's Word so that sin will not be crouching at our doors.

Here's a major concern: Will the "planes to catch and the bills to pay," as Harry Chapin's song chants, become the priorities in our lives? A young single mother recently shared the following frustration with me.

We wake up. The day begins. My child is changed, dressed, and fed. She is then placed in front of the TV to watch one of her favorite programs, a snack bowl on her lap. I have to answer my emails; I'm actively looking for a full-time job. Then I clean the kitchen, grab another cup of coffee before gathering laundry, feed and walk the dogs, and find another program for my child to watch while I make the beds and get dressed. One thing seems to lead to another and I never have time to just play and laugh with her. The demands of the day take over. It's frustrating.

Busy is a key word for parents today. Many young families are characterized by husbands and wives working outside the home. Little ones are enrolled in the best daycare facilities, sometimes even before they are born. There is a new phrase out there: bells and whistles. Young and growing families feel they must have them.

How sad that we see this in God's family also. This means hustle in the morning when everyone, including baby, is leaving the home. All family members are doing their own thing during the busiest, most productive part of the day, returning by late afternoon exhausted, but needing to plow through a quick dinner, often not together, so someone can be at soccer, baseball, or tennis practice. TV tells a story to little Johnny, and baby Sarah is entertained by the automatic swing before bath and sleep. Next morning it happens all over again as the alarm announces the start of a new day. Where is the quality time to listen, to respond, and to share insights into God's Word?

It's challenging for family members to even take time to look into one another's eyes and communicate instead of hearing a steady flow of directives from Dad or Mom.

As our children see how we walk in this world, they will have healthy models to follow.

Warm Is the Glowing

Warm is the home fires glowing
Where there is love—
Where all within the home
Seek power from above.

Warm is the home fires glowing
Where each one does his part—
To bring a spark of hope
To every dear one's heart.

Warm is the home fires glowing
Where kindness intercedes—
And every member strives
To meet each other's needs.

Warm is the home fires glowing
Where daily devotions are the key—
And prayer and Bible reading
Give strength to you and me.

Warm is the home fires glowing
Where Christ is King,
Father, mother, children—
To Him all praises bring.

Warm is the home fires glowing
Where no one cares to roam—
But all within its walls
Seek Heaven for their home.

—Judy Miller[1]

Serendipitous Mentoring by Dad

Our son John is all grown up. He has his own family. Every so often he'll pull into our driveway for a quick visit. Not a long one, but enough time to see how we are, to share a happening from his busy life, and then be on his way. My goodbye hug sounds something like this: "Love you, son. You're a good man. Keep James 1:19 close to you at work today." We laugh. How did he become this man?

There's an old newspaper photo of John as a four-year-old standing with his dad on the shore of a lake. It was raining so the reporter/photographer made it look like a silhouette, father and son holding fishing poles under a large umbrella. It's priceless to me. Quality time with Dad. John still remembers that day. I don't know what they talked about as he learned to cast and wait patiently, but this I do know: he has grown to be just like his dad. He purposes private time with two active young children, helping them learn how to rake and garden, throw that ball, and play geocache. I had to look this one up. It's a fun use of technology with parent and child working together to find a treasure. Yes, he's tired after a long day at school, but he values his role as "Daddy" and sees the importance of capturing those teachable moments. Deuteronomy 6:1–9 is still vitally important as his young ones grow toward their own accountability.

> *For where your treasure is, there*
> *your heart will be also.*
> —Matthew 6:21

A Memory That Mentored

Recently our daughter called to talk with her father. She lamented about her busy schedule each day, which did not allow for individual private time with her three children. They are in the midst of those wonder years called adolescence. She felt as though time was slipping by, days upon days, where she did

71

not have opportunity to just sit and talk, and most importantly, listen. It was a great concern to her.

Her father reminded her of the day she was called from her fifth-grade classroom to come to the office. He met her at the entrance and announced that they were going out for lunch. He also reminded her of how her face lit up with excitement and wonder. Dad had taken time from his busy day to take Chrissy out to lunch. The neighborhood Friendly's restaurant offered a quick and child-friendly menu. Off they went.

> She had learned to hold her tongue on giving advice, even when it was solicited.

"How you doing today, Chrissy?" was all it took to get the conversation flowing. A nod, a timely comment, and eye-to-eye contact sealing the message: You are important; I'm listening.

Many times during these special interludes, her father was able to share a story from his life, as well as a godly principle that Chrissy could take back to school with her. Forty minutes—that's all. But priceless in value.

How difficult is it for us to claim control of our busy day and make special private times with our children? Do we see it as something of great value? A wise older woman once shared that if something is a priority, we find a way to get it done. I believe she is right.

Our love for the Lord and following His commands should first be in our hearts. Then they can be practiced in our homes and consequently become habits that are comfortable and fulfilling to us and allow for godly goal-setting with our children. Finding those nuggets of time and opportunities to share meaningful insights is the key to the strong family units God knows we need. The trick is not to make them forced, but to make them a natural part of our time with our children. It is part of the outflow of our hearts.

Our daughter ended her phone call to drive over to the school and take her nine-year-old daughter out for lunch. I am happy to report that all went well, and she relived the joy of that long-ago young girl as she saw the smile on her own daughter's face.

The Back Door Plan

For several months Dorothy experienced lengthy phone conversations with her daughter, Jade Anne, who lived two thousand miles away. Her daughter's marriage was in turmoil. Dorothy provided a listening ear and timely validation of feelings. She had learned to hold her tongue on giving advice, even when it was solicited. One of those phone calls brought joy to Dorothy's heart as her daughter shared an insight, one she had just realized.

> Mom, you have listened to me, validated my feelings, even prayed with me on the phone. You have only given advice when I have asked, and then, generic in nature, your counsel continues to point me to consider what is true, not what my feelings dictate.
>
> You have sent the message: *You are important to me.* You haven't just said it; you have done it in the gift of time. In short, you have modeled for me how I need to be with my daughter. It's imperative for me to spend that kind of quality time with her, letting her know by my example how important she is to me. I can't just trust that it will happen; I need to purpose it.

Dorothy prayed a silent prayer of thanksgiving to God. To frame this insight from her daughter properly, one needs to understand that Dorothy yearned to be that older woman who could mentor her married children, especially in things pertaining to their children. However, wisdom dictated following healthy boundaries and being supportive when asked. Over and over Dorothy recognized how God provided ways. She called it her "back-door entries" where she could influence quietly, gently, and thoughtfully without fanfare. She sent more silent thanks to God and then allowed one further validation to Jade Anne.

> You could not have said anything more precious to me. Thank you. I encourage you to act on this insight to purpose special time with your sweet

two-year-old. I know that you will have fun as you set aside your busy schedule to include this.

How parents claim time and purpose time with their children is up to them. Here are a few practical ideas for intentional parenting.

- See the need.
- Do not procrastinate.
- Look for opportunities and follow through.

Again, I quote a wise grandma who said, "People usually do what's important to them." Let's be honest about where our priorities rest. May they be according to God's will.

Christian Books That Mentor

Sheila Keckler Butt wrote the book *No Greater Joy*. The book is easy reading and entertaining. Sheila is the mother of three grown sons who have been raised in a Christian environment. Their daddy is a preacher. One particular story in Sheila's book lends itself to the theme of this chapter: finding nuggets of time where you can have meaningful, even God-focused one-on-one time with your child.

> I know of a father who gives each of his two teenagers a blessing every night. He asks the Lord to bless them during a test the next day, or during a track meet, or in some other of their important endeavors. When their fifteen-year-old son spends a night away from home, he calls to talk to his father and ask what his blessing is for the evening. What a beautiful relationship in the Lord![2]

And what do you suppose that young man will do with his children when he eventually has his own family?

I love reading parenting books that give practical advice to mothers and fathers. We are blessed with resources at our fingertips. My concern: Do parents take the time to read these insightful mentoring books? And further, do they make the obvious connections in their own lives?

Many Christian women have shared their wisdom through writing. What an expedient way to reach countless numbers of women looking for advice. A book I will always cherish is Betty Bender's *To Love a Child.* A mother of three grown, believing children, wife of a gospel preacher, teacher of women's classes, guest speaker at retreats, author of several books, and certainly a lifelong student of God's Word, Betty shares parenting insights in a forthright way, telling it like it is. She makes no apologies for her often-blunt statements, but rather backs them up with actual case studies of people she has known. Two chapters that relate nicely to this theme of taking the much-needed time with our children are titled "Get the Family Together" and "Establish Family Traditions."[3]

Let's be honest about where our priorities rest. May they be according to God's will.

Betty Bender reminded me of a time when our daughter and her family were visiting with us from Minnesota. Her husband's son Nick had joined us too. It was Nick's thirteenth birthday, and we made a proper fuss over him. When we brought out the dried navy beans and gave each member at the table three beans, Nick thought we had lost it. He wasn't very thrilled when we announced "The Bean Game," where each person at the table shared a memory about Nick or complimented him on some part of his life, placing a bean in the decorated bowl. Before we began Nick said, "This is silly." However, once started, everyone saw his countenance gradually lift. When he heard the last memory, which, by the way, was very funny, he said, "Let's do that again!"

Never lose sight of the importance of acknowledging one another with happy uplifting comments and expressing our appreciation and love. Ephesians 4:29 tells us that our words should serve to edify and give grace to those who hear. It should be a priority for us as we strive to build strong families. And yes, it does take purposed time. Invaluable purposed time. Be intentional.

Let no unwholesome word proceed from your mouth, but only such a word as is good for edification according to the need of the moment, so that it will give grace to those who hear (Ephesians 4:29).

Technology Is Here

The scene was at the Tampa Airport. Frank and I had about an hour before boarding our plane for home. Very predictably I walked to my favorite coffee shop and took my place in a long line. Looking again at the line, I quickly realized that we all could have been part of an Apple or Samsung commercial. Everyone in line, yes, even me, was gazing intently at his or her smart phone. I started to look around at those passing by. What I saw was astounding. People were either looking at their phones or talking into them as they hurried to their gates. A mother, talking on her phone, pushed a stroller with a child of about three. The child was gazing intently at an iPad, using her little fingers to swipe and touch. I was stunned to see in this very impromptu study that most of the people were engaged with techno devices. I slipped my phone quietly into my purse after turning it completely off. After paying for the coffee, I returned to Frank, but not before scrutinizing our whole sitting area. And, yes, most were using either computers or phones, or reading from Kindle screens. Only a few were actually having conversations. Frank and I were among them.

Whether we like it or not, technology is here to stay and has become increasingly more available to us. Television, internet, video games, iPads, cell phones—all with the abilities to be either incredibly useful or harmful and addicting. It's up to the individual to determine how technology will flavor his life. Furthermore, it's imperative for parents to manage wisely how their children engage with technology.

Many articles share the good, the bad, and the ugly of technology. The following is paraphrased information that came from a study released in May 2013 and titled "The Impact of Technology on the Developing Child."[4]

In a 2010 study, the Kaiser Foundation found that the average school-aged child spent seven and a half hours per day watching television. Seventy-five percent of those studied allowed television in their children's bedrooms, and fifty percent left the television on all day. Since this report is dated, it would not be surprising to find that the stats have increased in favor of more hours with techno devices, especially video games on iPads and computers as well as television.

Here's the result that doctors and psychologists, including counselors, have found regarding the children they service and the direct correlation to techno devices. There has been an increase of physical, psychological, and behavioral disorders, along with increased cases of childhood diabetes and obesity. Conditions such as ADHD, autism, coordination disorders, and developmental delays are on the rise. That's just for starters.

If we do not think techno devices influence our children and how they see this world and the values they are formulating, we are sadly mistaken. It is up to each of us to handle technology wisely and with respect. Before purchasing one of these "toys" for preschool and school-aged children, it is imperative that parents read articles such as the above and be proactive about how these toys will be used, especially at home.

By the way, this plan is more successful if parents are honest about how much they are involved with techno devices during a typical day. What does their model look like to their children? And truthfully, how much one-on-one time with their children is being robbed because it is easier to let technology babysit and entertain? Where are our priorities? God's priorities haven't changed. He still calls us to love and honor Him first. He calls us to share with our children. Parents may need to do some honest reflecting and changing. The key is to be

> If we do not think techno devices influence our children and how they see this world and the values they are formulating, we are sadly mistaken.

proactive about how technology will impact your home. The flip side is to plan quality time with your children that requires you to move, touch, connect, and enjoy nature and to have some active sweat-producing play. And as opportunities arise, share an insight about the Lord.

My Prayer

Father, in this busy world, may today's parents find quality time to engage with their children in meaningful ways, ways that will influence their children to know You and to be guided by Your love. Help parents be creative in finding time to actively listen, to play, and to pray with their children while their window of time is still open. And please help them to be wise in the use of all the technology tools that are so available. Bless them with wisdom, energy, creativity, and a desire to please You, as they reprioritize their busy lives to include those precious one-on-one interludes. In the name of Jesus, Amen.

Have a Good Time Now: Activities for Opportunities

Below are just a few activities for younger children that certainly can be modified to use with your child. Hopefully they will trigger more ideas and many hours of quality time with your youngster.

- *Rainy-Day Splash:* On a rainy day, gather your children and say, "Put on your boots, grab an umbrella, and let's go walk in the puddles." (You might want to establish some easy umbrella rules.) Then splash about, not worrying about getting wet. Sing an appropriate song as you banter or discover what worms do on rainy days. Be sure to practice respect for nature's small creatures. Make clean-up easy by having changes of clothing ready, along with a special treat. Give thanks to God for what you did.

- *Pretend with Play Dough:* Find a good recipe for play dough. Make it together and take time to play with your child. It's amazing how quickly a little one will listen to your made-up story and mimic it to tell her own version.

    Two-year-old Danielle and I made the plates and cookies for a play dough tea party. We then invited her favorite "Noah's Ark Animals" (small rubber animals) to come to the party. *Please* and *thank you* were key words.

- *Walking Journal:* Have a drawing tablet handy that can serve as a journal of special walks you and your child take. Even five minutes outside might allow you to watch a butterfly land on a flower or to find a colorful leaf. Any "find" can become the easy theme of a page in the drawing journal. A few choice written words make the memory last and readable to your youngster. God's creation offers so much!

> It is up to each of us to handle technology wisely and with respect.

- *Sink Splash:* Fill a plastic or metal mixing bowl with warm water and place it in the kitchen sink. Think through how your child can stand at the sink safely on a chair or stool. And here's the key! You stay there too! Play with your child, letting him/her lead. At times you can initiate something new, like rain, using a spray bottle, thanking God for the rain.

- *Tent Story Time:* Build a tent with blankets between pulled-out chairs or with part of the couch. Crawl in with your child and read a story together.

- *Picnic with Nature Lessons:* Plan a picnic lunch, go for a walk, and spread a blanket. Have lunch together out in God's world.

- *Campfire at Home:* If you have a fire pit in your back yard, build a "campfire" and eat hot dogs roasted on sticks. Make smores together and sing camp songs. (Do you think King David sat with his men around campfires?)

- *More Resources:* The internet is bursting with ideas just waiting to be shared. Google the phrase: *Easy activities with young children.*

    Bob Keeshan, TV's Captain Kangaroo, authored a book called *Family Fun Activities Book*. It's filled with activities geared to bring children and grownups together.

Interacting with Older Children

Older children need parental time in different ways. Consider the following ideas for interaction.

- *Before Bedtime:* Take time to listen to your children before bedtime. Validate their feelings, giving them the silent message that their feelings are important to you. End with simple prayers of thanksgiving.

- *TV Together:* Watch television programs together and discuss anything controversial. Be a good listener and value their comments. Use scripture sparingly, yet effectively to make a simple point. Wait for comments.

- *Get Outside:* Go out and throw that ball around, Dad or Mom! Or play soccer in the rain.

- *Technology Togetherness:* Do a "geocache" together. Your older child might have to instruct you! This could lead to a discussion about "The Pearl of Great Price."

- *Eat Together:* Make dinner time a priority and eat together. The food isn't as important as the conversation. I know of a family who posts a topic on a chart near the dining table. The family is preset for conversation. Or make a date for lunch and be prompt for pick-up time to and from school.

- *Read Aloud, Pray Aloud:* Find a mutually chosen chapter book and read aloud to your children. We went through all of C. S. Lewis's *The Chronicles of Narnia* together. The school or community librarian can direct you to books or resources. Pray together before leaving for school or work. Be specific in your requests for each child.

- *Bible Timeline:* A Bible timeline stationed conveniently in the home can help facilitate quick references to Bible facts.

- *More Resources:* The internet has a plethora of ideas for having purposed quality time with your older children.

Young Parents' Prayer
They're Only Little Once

Grant me the wisdom to guide them down the path that their feet
  should take,
For I know that they can never turn back and walk those paths
  with me again.
Give me the wisdom to guide their feet so that someday they'll be
  able to walk alone;
They're only little once.

Give me the time I need to enjoy them,
For I know that after they're grown
I'll never have another chance to tell stories and pretend at those
  tea parties.
I'll never have another chance to watch them in a school play or
  church sing,
or to see them catch that first fish or hit that first home run ball.
Give me the time in life's busy schedule to have fun with my
  children.
They're only little once.

Let me be a loving parent.
Let me correct and not punish, explain and not merely scold.
Let me know when to correct, and how often, and when it's best
  to just look the other way.
Help me be patient and give me a gentle hand to mold them into
  better people.
They're only little once.

Let me be a good teacher and an even better example.
Give me the right words and deeds to teach them.
Grant me the key to unlock their spirits and set them truly free,
For they're only little one time,
Only innocent and trusting and pliable for a space of time,
One minute in an eternity.
Let me do my best for them while I have the chance.

—Author Unknown[5]

It's Your Turn

1. Google simple activities to do with children. Make sure of the following:

   - Age-appropriate to your children

   - Easy to plan / facilitate

   - Does not cost money

   - Practice / review it first. Be excited about it. Have reflection time afterward with your children.

   - Listen carefully and validate their thoughts.

2. Research and review the lyrics of the 1974 song "The Cat's in the Cradle" by Harry Chapin. How might you be drawn into this same situation? How might you prevent it?

3. Find television shows that can be viewed by the whole family and promote discussion about appropriate / inappropriate behaviors. If you cannot find any, go to the local library and look through the DVD section. View them with some specific listening purposes in mind. (This means you have to preview before everyone watches.)

4. What is one new way that you can spend quality time with your children? How can you be purposeful in scheduling this special time?

5. Write down each of your children's names and one thing that you want to pray about for each child. Get into the practice of praying with them about their special needs and cares.

6. In this fast-paced culture, multi-tasking is the norm. Often you get involved in activities that you consider very important that demand your total focus. When your preschooler or toddler enters the scene seeking your company and relentlessly vying for your full attention, frustration knocks on your door. What can you do to make this a win-win situation?

7. "The real responsibility we have as parents is to be the kind of parents we want our children to be." Comment on this statement. Be specific in stating one way you do this.

8. What are your "bells and whistles"? How does affording them take away from or add to your relationships with your children?

9. Relate one example of how you live Deuteronomy 6:6–7 before your children. What do you do specifically?

Judy grew up in Arkansas and Mississippi and married her high school sweetheart, Bob, more than fifty years ago. They moved nineteen times through five states in fifty-four years. They have three sons and daughters-in-law and seven grandchildren. She has taught children from cradle roll to teens and also ladies' classes. Judy enjoys reading, gardening, oil painting, sewing, and refinishing and restoring furniture. Her main joy is the Lord, and next to that, her family. 🌼

Chapter 7

Mentor Me, I'm a Mother-in-Law

by Judy Cofer

Separating the topics of mothers-in-law and daughters-in-law is an impossible assignment. They are intertwined. If you are a mother-in-law, read into the next chapter for more insight.

Adam and Eve were the happiest and most blessed people in the world. Why? Because neither of them had a mother-in-law! Mothers-in-law have been the brunt of many jokes since jokes began. Usually the wife's mother is the one the joke focuses on, but it can also be the husband's mother. Can you connect with these?

- My mother-in-law's other car is a broom!

- My mother-in-law is a well-balanced person. She's got a chip on both shoulders.

- I wouldn't say that my mother-in-law is ugly, but every time she puts on lipstick, it tries to crawl back into the tube.

We laugh at these jokes, but it is not so funny when you are the mother-in-law.

A Complicated Relationship

Mothers-in-law, like all of us, come with many different personalities. Some are sweet and some not so sweet. Some are difficult to get along with; others are easy to be with. Some want to please; others want to be pleased.

For many reasons, the mother-in-law and daughter-in-law relationship can be complicated. Many factors contribute to this very special relationship. It may be that both families have unrealistic expectations. Sometimes both sets of parents seem to think their adult child's choice of a mate is not good enough. They are different. Or perhaps the parents make up their minds prematurely not to like the choice their child makes. Here's an example.

> Suzie is finally engaged and is excited to introduce her future husband to her mother. She says, "Mom, I am going to bring home three guys. I want you to guess which one I am going to marry."
>
> Later, Suzie walks in with three guys following her. Without blinking an eye, her mother points to one and says, "It is that one."
>
> "Wow," exclaims Suzie, "How in the world did you know it was him?"
>
> "I just do not like him!" her mother replied.

Again we laugh. But are we guilty of this kind of thinking? As parents, ask yourselves these questions regarding your expectations of a future son-in-law or daughter-in-law:

- Do we expect our child's choice to think like we think?
- Do we expect our child's choice to have a personality like ours?
- Do we expect our child's choice to have no flaws? (Probably not, because we can readily see their flaws.)
- Is our child perfect? Be honest!

As we begin this study about relationships between daughters-in-law and mothers-in-law, it is a good time to apply God's Word about the fruit of the spirit: Love, joy, peace, patience, kindness, goodness, faithfulness, gentleness, and self-control (Galatians 5:22–23). If we allow God's Spirit to control us adding these characteristics, will not our actions toward one another, especially daughters- and sons-in-law, reflect love and peace and patience?

My Three Sons

I am the mother of three sons and now mother-in-law to three daughters-in-law. When I was raising my sons, there was one thing foremost in my heart. I wanted them to grow up to be men who loved God and be godly husbands and fathers. I remember praying specifically for their future wives. I realized if they chose a mate who did not love God and want to obey Him, the family's hearts could be influenced away from God.

During their teenage years, my sons' world of influence began to expand beyond our home environment and beyond the impact of godly friends and relatives. They experienced peer pressure. There was the desire for independence, although I knew their young minds were not mature enough to be independent. I remembered those feelings of desiring independence. Do you? It was exciting.

But I also knew some influences could be destructive to their young bodies, minds,

It may be that both families have unrealistic expectations. Sometimes both sets of parents seem to think their adult child's choice of a mate is not good enough.

and souls. My husband and I strove diligently to teach and discipline them in the Lord. And we went to "the begging place" before our Father. There were times that I needed knee pads! As I prayed, I wanted God to answer me immediately. I would say, "Where are you, God? Tell me what to do!" Then in studying Hebrews, I realized that God was speaking to me when He said, "I will never leave you nor forsake you" (Hebrews 13:5 NKJV). I was reminded of a comment my mother handed down from our wise brother, Marshall Keeble: "If you do not know which way to go, stand still awhile," which was certainly an application of the scripture, "Be still and know that I am God" (Psalm 46:10 NKJV).

The Influence of the World

Consider the following proverbs: "A wise son makes a father glad, but a foolish son is a grief to his mother" (Proverbs 10:1), and "A wise son makes a father glad, but a foolish man despises his mother" (Proverbs 15:20).

Isn't it interesting that these proverbs describe the effects a foolish man has on his mother? He is no longer a child but a man persisting in living foolishly. Remember the parable of the lost son in Luke 15:11–32? Although this son was not influenced by a wife, he was influenced by worldly pleasures. The scriptures do not tell us about the effect this lost son had on his mother, but we can speculate. She must have been brokenhearted. However, the words do paint a picture of a father who was watching for his son's return. When he saw him coming, he ran to meet him. There was great celebration. That is a view of our heavenly Father watching over His children, even allowing them to leave Him but constantly watching for their return. What an example for us parents!

> "If you do not know which way to go, stand still awhile."
>
> –Marshall Keeble

We mothers know our sons will leave us some day and be joined to a wife. We want him to be a man who will not be influenced by worldly pleasures. We want him to love his wife with all his heart. We want him to guide his family in God's way. And we know for him to do this, we must turn him loose. We must allow him to leave but it is not easy.

Roots and Wings

Prominent newspaper editor and journalist Hodding Carter quoted a wise woman's saying,

> There are only two lasting bequests we can hope to give our children. One of these is roots; the other, wings. They can only be grown, these roots and

wings, in the home. We want our sons' roots to grow deep into the soil beneath them and into the past, not in arrogance but in confidence.[1]

Leaving and Cleaving

Adam and Eve did not have earthly parents. God created Adam from the dust of the ground and made Eve from Adam's rib. He presented her to Adam. How did Adam react?

> "This is now bone of my bones, and flesh of my flesh; she shall be called Woman, because she was taken out of Man." For this reason a man shall leave his father and his mother, and be joined to his wife; and they shall become one flesh (Genesis 2:23–24).

The source of the last part of that verse is probably an insert God instructed Moses to write. If they were Adam's own words, where did he get the information? He had no earthly parents to leave. God would have had to give those thoughts and instructions to him. However God did it, He thought it important for husband and wife from the very beginning to have instructions from Him concerning the importance of forming a separate family unit from the parents. Leave and cleave.

- As parents, we need to let our children form that unit.
- There must be a leaving before there can be a cleaving.

> There shall be, by the order of God, a more intimate connection formed between the man and woman, than can subsist even between parents and children.[2]

Note Matthew Henry's observations on Genesis 2:24:

1. To whom can we more firmly bond than the fathers that begat us and the mothers who bore us? Yet the son must quit them to be joined to his wife, and the daughter must forget them to cleave to her husband.

2. See how necessary it is that children should take their parents' consent along with them in their marriage, and how unjust those are to their

parents, as well as undutiful, who marry without it, for they rob them of their right to them and interest in them and alienate it to another, fraudulently and unnaturally.

3. See what need there is both of prudence and prayer in the choice of this relation, which is so near and so lasting. That had need be well done which is to be done for life.

4. See how firm the bond of marriage is, not to be divided and weakened by having many wives or to be broken or cut off by divorce for any cause but fornication.

5. See how dear the affection ought to be between husband and wife, such as there is to our own bodies. These two are one flesh. Let them be one soul.[3]

When Does Leaving and Cleaving Begin?

Do you remember when your first child was born? You marveled at that perfect gift from God and observed with pride and delight each new accomplishment and the natural growth of your precious baby. Although many years passed before your child became independent, the leaving began at birth. The baby left the security, warmth, and care of your womb and had to breathe on his own. There would be many more "leavings" before maturity. Remember when you had to leave him at kindergarten? It seemed only a short time and he was graduating high school and leaving for college. Those "leavings" were natural and good.

But what if your child had not been healthy or able to leave in the natural way? I have a cousin who has cerebral palsy. There were signs of physical problems, but they were not so apparent until she began to crawl. Instead of crawling on her hands and knees like other children, Jennifer began to pull herself along with her arms, dragging the rest of her body, not using her legs. We children made a game of crawling with Jennifer the way she crawled. My aunt and uncle took her to many doctors and finally got the diagnosis—Jennifer would not develop normally. Her reading skills would be minimal. Neither would she walk. Jennifer spent her waking hours in a wheelchair, but she was loved by all our family. She enjoyed being teased by her uncles and cousins.

Jennifer is now in her late sixties and makes her home in a nursing facility. She delights the other residents with her joyful visits each morning. She enjoys making pot holders to share with her cousins—she has several. Her one hundred-year-old mother, who taught her to read, lives down the hall.

When our children begin to establish their own families, we must remember that process is built into their brains by the Master Builder. Leaving parents and cleaving to a spouse is natural. It is time for parents to step back and allow God to be in control. Unless there is a disability that prevents their leaving, it is unusual for them to remain with us. It is time for them to leave and cleave to their spouse. How thankful we should be that they can leave their parents and live on their own. Yes, we will miss them, but as Grand Ole Opry comedian Jerry Clower used to say, "Do not worry about your children leaving your home. They are coming back and bringing more with them."

He is acquiring another family, not just a spouse.

The Other Family

When your child finds the one he wants to marry, he is acquiring another family, not just a spouse. When meeting the other parents, he naturally wants to be on his best behavior. He wants to impress the new in-laws. But it is important to give him this advice: Be yourself. If you are naturally quiet and reserved, do not try to be anything else. If your personality is outgoing, let that trait shine through. Be the real you.

> The masking of oneself can become a serious source of distress in one's life. In fact, it contributes to most of our problems. We conceal our true identity and mask what we really are, whether good or bad. We hesitate to reveal our true selves for fear of what others might think of us. If we are going to have

good solid relationships with God and others, we have to take off the masks. We have to come to grips with realness. We have to become authentic.[4]

It is equally important for prospective parents-in-law to be genuine also. "Faking it" to impress will only add to the stress of the young couple. You want love, acceptance, and warmth to rule in your home and in theirs.

Keeping the Distance

In the 1970s we knew a young couple who, because of their career, had moved a long distance from both sets of parents. The young man had a great fear of crossing bridges. He sometimes traveled a longer route just to avoid a bridge. To emphasize the value of moving away from both sets of parents, he often said, "Young couples should move five hundred miles and three bridges away from their parents."

> The responsibility to leave and cleave is a responsibility for the parents also.

I have often wondered why he felt that way. Could it be that he and his wife were learning many valuable lessons of independence away from parental influences? Could it be they were learning to depend on each other and make decisions without input from either set of parents?

In reality, not everyone can move five hundred miles and three bridges away from parents, but with God's help any couple can leave parents and cleave to one another. But we should remember this: The responsibility to leave and cleave is a responsibility for the parents also. We must let our children leave us and cleave to each other. That is God's plan for each couple. God even brought the leaving/cleaving scripture of Genesis into the New Testament for us. "For this cause shall a man leave his father and mother, and shall cleave to his wife; and the two shall become one flesh" (Ephesians 5:31 ASV).

Mothers of Sons or Daughters

Another expression we often hear is this: "When your daughter marries, you have many responsibilities. But when your son marries, you have only three things to do: Buy a new girdle, get your hair done, and keep your mouth shut.

We laugh at this advice, especially the "girdle" part. Perhaps it's true for so many mothers of sons. But being a mother of sons only, this was not my experience. All three of my daughters-in-law included me in many aspects of their weddings. I cherish those memories and their kind hearts toward me.

Mother-in-Law to Mother-in-Law

When I asked mothers to share their experiences of becoming a mother-in-law, I also asked them to share some things they have learned that would be helpful to other mothers in navigating those sometimes turbulent waters we all tread in becoming a peaceful family. Here is their advice:

- Do not be hurt when your daughter-in-law shows favoritism to her family. It is only natural. They are blood relatives. That also goes for a son-in-law. They do not mean to exclude you.

- Encourage your daughter or son in the new marriage relationship by stepping back. Give the young couple space to grow together. Untie the apron strings. Give them wings. Their focus now should be on each other and their family, not on you.

    Do not do anything to interfere with the decisions they make together. They are a separate home now. Be loving, supportive, kind, and helpful. But do not offer unsolicited advice or help.

- Do not expect your daughter-in-law or son-in-law to include you in every activity in their home. They need time with their younger friends. Remember also that they do not feel you must invite them every time you have your friends over.

- Do not ask questions about finances or other personal matters. If your son or daughter begins to "confide" those matters to you, change the subject.

93

You do not need to know those things. Our children need to be depending on each other, not on us. One of the responses from daughters-in-law expressed that very problem.

- Depending on the individual situation, it may be wise to visit their homes only when invited. We do not want to "wear out our welcome."

- When the family includes children, follow the advice of my wise mentor, Betty Bender, who says, "Let your children raise their children. Do not constantly be in their home or have them in yours, although it is tempting for getting the grands' sweet hugs." Ask the parents' permission before offering food or toys to the children.

- New parents are especially particular about nutrition and are more aware of the kinds of toys that are safe. Follow the mother's instructions when you babysit. They know what is best for their child and will appreciate your attention to their desires.

I am adding my advice to theirs. Even though we fully intend to include our in-laws as our own children, consider these objectives.

1. *Be careful.* The in-laws may perceive that you are trying to "mother" them with your words and actions. They might conclude that you want to take the place of their mother, regardless of your motive.

2. *Do not try to change them.* Just love them.

3. *Realize that you will make mistakes.* When you do blunder, learn from it.

4. *Pray.* Ask God to guide you. Ask your family to pray for you. Let them see your love and sincere concern for them. When you make mistakes, let your words and actions convey your repentance. Ask forgiveness.

I have learned so much from my daughters-in law, and I am still learning. The experience of being a mother-in-law is still new to me, and I am so grateful for the patience my daughters-in-law show to me. Thank you, Stephanie, Delisa, and Vickie. I love you all.

Numerous scriptures can guide us to be better in-laws and grandparents. Here are two that are especially applicable.

- "Let every man be swift to hear, slow to speak, slow to wrath" (James 1:19 NKJV).
- "Whoever guards his mouth and his tongue keeps his soul from troubles" (Proverbs 21:23 NKJV).

Summary

When I began writing about the unique experiences of mother-in-law / daughter-in-law relationships, I was not sure how to express my thoughts. Could I express my love for my daughters-in-law and let them get a glimpse into my heart as to how it feels to be a mother of sons and to be a mother-in-law? I decided to ask other women their thoughts.

One mother-in-law expressed the following frustration. She was not bitter or hurt. She was just asking why.

> Facebook is a powerful thing. We did not have Facebook when our family was young so we expressed our feelings and ideas in letters or by conversation or by thoughtful deeds. I recall sitting with my children and helping them write letters to their grandparents. And when we wrote to my parents, we also wrote to my husband's parents. When we displayed pictures, they were of both sets of grandparents. I understand it is only natural to think of your own parents first, but I wanted our children to learn to be thoughtful to both, not showing what might appear as favoritism.
>
> But I have noticed that is not the case with my daughter-in-law. Her Facebook page has many pictures of her siblings and parents, which is understandable and a good thing. But I also notice that there are none of her husband's parents and very few of our side of the family. It appears to me we are a non-entity.

Among those who responded to my inquiries were career women, stay-at-home moms, and grandmothers. Some lived far away; some lived near. There were mothers of daughters and mothers of sons. All were Christians; that was the common thread. Here is a summary of their feelings.

We want you, our daughters-in-law or sons-in-law, present or future, to know that we raised our sons and daughters with the future and you in our thoughts. We prayed for you before we knew you. We prayed we were raising our sons and daughters to be the best helpers in your Christian walk together. We still pray for you. And we ask you to pray for us. Ask God to give us wisdom, patience, and pleasant words to share. "Pleasant words are a honeycomb, sweet to the soul and healing to the bones" (Proverbs 16:24). Those are our desires. We love you and want to be your friend.

It's Your Turn

1. Why are mothers-in-law the brunt of so many jokes?

2. What can we do to prepare our children for leaving us?

3. What does leaving involve?

4. After our children leave us and begin their homes, develop family traditions, and make new friends, how can we make the transition easier? List two *dos* and *don'ts*.

5. After giving children roots, why is it so difficult to give them wings?

6. What words or actions from a parent might make the leaving and cleaving process more difficult for grown children? Give an example.

7. Since cleaving is part of the leaving process, what does "cleaving" mean? Cleave to what or to whom? Why?

8. How can we prevent crowding our children's marriages by becoming a third presence?

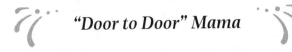

"Door to Door" Mama

God sent me to you; will you let me come in?
I'm a "door to door" Mama, on needles and pins.
I don't want to pressure, just help with your load.
It's God's way of service; I'll not be a goad
Or a scolder or a cause of distress—
But rather a friend who understands the mess with which
Satan entraps us by his desire for our soul.
We want heaven, but that's not his goal.
Together let's reason and read from God's Word and
Learn all the lessons yet to be heard.
We'll pray for endurance and take a long look at the
Wealth of the answers found in the Book.

—Lea Fowler

Quoting Scripture is the easy part. Living Scripture is sometimes hard. How many marriages would improve if each partner took seriously the charge not to "take into account a wrong suffered" (1 Corinthians 13:5)? Other translations say that love "keeps no records of wrongs." It is easy to talk about love, but we want to practice love. When we're exasperated with our "in-law," we should not whip out a ledger sheet of every wrong action. We can learn to be patient and kind. It is not easy, but it is worth it.

—Judy Cofer

Chapter 8

Mentor Me, I'm a Daughter-in-Law

by Judy Cofer

Separating the topics of mother-in-law from daughter-in-law is an impossible assignment. They are intertwined. I'm repeating this sentence because someone might pick out this chapter only and then miss the perspective of the previous chapter. Read that one too.

I recently read a blog by a mother who began praying for the mothers of her future daughters-in-law and sons-in-law when she rocked and held her babies. The writer expressed thoughts that accurately reflected my own. After interviewing other mothers, I learned their thoughts were much the same.

It begins: "If my child marries yours . . . I just want you to know that I am praying for you."

> I am praying that you will hug your boy tight when he is sad or lonely or scared. Because, someday, my girl—all grown up and beautiful with babies of her own—will be sad or lonely or scared. And he will need to know how to hold her. Teach him.
>
> And let your daughters speak righteous words that bring life and hope. Because some day, my sons will be worn and weary, and the words you are placing in your daughters' minds today just might become the balm to my son's soul.
>
> I am doing my best to do the same. And sometimes—much of the time—I fail. Pray for me too.[1]

Learning to Leave and Love

The previous quote reminds me of our responsibility as mothers to be thinking of the future when our sons and daughters will exit our home, marry, and establish their own homes. We need to prepare them to leave.

Oriental customs during Bible times were very different from ours today, according to Fred H. Wight in *Manners and Customs of Bible Lands*. When a couple got married, the bridegroom would go to the home of the bride and bring her back to his house, or sometimes the bride's relatives would conduct her from her father's house to the house of her fiancé, where her new home was to be. Before leaving the house that had been her home, she would receive the blessing of her relatives.[2]

Did you ever wonder why Orpah and Ruth were living with Naomi, their mother-in-law? That was the custom. But after the deaths of their husbands and father-in-law, Naomi decided to return to Jerusalem. She told Ruth and Orpah to return to their parents' homes. We are not told anything about their families, but we can speculate that since the Moabites were idol worshipers and the family of Naomi were worshipers of God, the influence of a godly family had more influence on Ruth, as she chose to go with her mother-in-law. Because of her decision that day, Ruth, a Moabite, a Gentile, became the wife of Boaz, who was the son of Rahab from Jericho. She and Boaz became parents of Obed who was the father of Jesse who was the father of David and in the lineage of Jesus Christ.

The godly influence of Naomi is clearly seen in the advice she gave to Ruth. And the respect Ruth had for Naomi is evident in her accepting and following godly advice.

Ruth and Naomi are the perfect examples of the kind of relationship I want. Each woman I interviewed expressed her desire to have a daughter-in-law like Ruth. So how are we to achieve that? What are a mother-in-law and daughter-in-law to do? The Bible has answers, and a good place to begin is with the word *love*.

Love is patient, love is kind and is not jealous; love does not brag and is not arrogant, does not act unbecomingly; it does not seek its own, is not provoked, does not take into account a wrong suffered (1 Corinthians 13:4–5).

Quoting Scripture is the easy part. Living Scripture is sometimes hard. How many marriages would improve if each partner took seriously the charge not to "take into account a wrong suffered" (1 Corinthians 13:5)? Other translations say that love "keeps no records of wrongs." It is easy to talk about love, but we want to practice love. When we're exasperated with our "in-law," we should not whip out a ledger sheet of every wrong action. We can learn to be patient and kind. It is not easy, but it is worth it.

From "Mothers-in-Law about Daughters-in-Law" (from my surveys):

- "I have the best daughter-in-law. She loves my son with all her heart and her love was clearly evident as the family was getting ready to attend a formal function. When my son and daughter-in-law appeared, ready to go, I noticed my son's shoes were splattered with paint, so I said to him, 'You cannot wear those shoes. They have paint spots all over them.' Then looking at my son with love written all over her face, my daughter-in-law replied, 'Isn't he wonderful. You can see by looking at his shoes that he is an artist.' I silently thanked God for giving my son such an adoring wife."

Kindness is the language which the deaf can hear and the blind can see.
—Anonymous

- "I thought we had the perfect friendship for a soon-to-be daughter-in-law and mother-in-law. We had many common interests and enjoyed doing things together. One of those interests was antiques, hers about a decade younger than mine. But we each saw potential in the restoration of old furniture, so we enjoyed searching thrift shops and visiting garage sales for just the right piece. My future daughter-in-law often invited me to lunch.

We even had careers in the same field which allowed us to have good conversations about our work.

I knew the relationship would change after she and my son married. Then, instead of spending some free time with me, she would want to be with her husband. I was pleased to see her attention devoted to him. I remembered the 'leaving and cleaving' scripture of Ephesians 5:31 and could see, as husband and wife, the cleaving process was beginning.

But I was not prepared to be viewed as an enemy or a competitor, and that seemed to be happening. Suddenly, my thoughts on furniture restoration were all wrong. I should be painting my furniture the same way she did hers. Restoration was the old way of doing it. I learned to be quiet and prayed for patience."

Mothers of engaged sons are often told: "When your son is getting married and you come to his wedding, wear beige and keep your mouth shut!" We laugh at such expressions, but one mother, whose first son was getting married, simply replied, "I am not wearing beige!"

> *Walk . . . worthy . . . with all humility*
> *and gentleness, with patience, bearing*
> *with one another in love.*
> —Ephesians 4:1–2 ESV

- "My precious daughter-in-law often sends me a sweet card. And many of them express appreciation to me for raising a son who is a loving husband and father. What kind words from my daughter-in-law. I cherish every card."

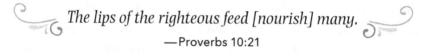

> *The lips of the righteous feed [nourish] many.*
> —Proverbs 10:21

One mother who responded spoke of her surprise to learn about "girl drama." She was a mother to sons only. She expressed her feelings frankly.

• "I was having lunch with my future daughter-in-law and the conversation turned to the wedding plans about colors, food, flowers, and other details. In our discussion I did not mean to be suggesting she do her wedding a certain way, but that is the way she perceived it. That night, my son came to me with reprimands, 'Mother, do not talk about our wedding details. I know what you mean, but she doesn't.' And that issue with her did not easily die. I quickly learned not to offer ideas. I had experienced my introduction to 'girl drama'! Having raised only boys, that experience was a great awakening for me."

Whoever guards his mouth and tongue
keeps his soul from troubles.
—**Proverbs 21:23** NKJV

Daughters-in-Law, It's Your Turn

Just as I asked for opinions from mothers-in-law, I also asked daughters-in-law for their thoughts. Here are some of them.

"My mother-in-law and I have so much fun together. She was my friend before she was my mother-in-law. She even introduced me to her son. And now that we have children, she never interferes by offering unsolicited advice about how we should be raising them. She will express an opinion, but only if I ask. Then I can depend on her words to be truthful and framed with kindness and a loving attitude."

"I try very hard to be a daughter-in-law that my in-laws love. And I think they love me, although they never express it to me or encourage me. I do, however, hear about the things I do wrong or different from their way of doing things. For instance, when they visit us, my mother-in-law tells me I am cooking too much food or not enough food. When we visit them, I feel I should help with meals or with other tasks. But she always criticizes me about what I do or how I do it. So I have stopped trying to help. Now I am reprimanded because 'I am just letting her wait on me.'"

Careful with fire is good advice we know.
Careful with words is ten times doubly so.
—William Carleton

"I had a great mother-in-law. When her son and I were planning our wedding, she volunteered to sew my wedding dress. It was beautiful! When we had our family, my mother-in-law helped in so many ways. She loved to cook, so she prepared many meals for us. She loved babysitting the grandchildren and enjoyed playing games with them. I worked outside our home, and her help was very much appreciated. She exemplified the traits I hope I can imitate in being a mother-in-law."

"My experience with my mother-in-law has been a good one over-all, but there was a time when I did not appreciate her wanting to know all our business, including financial. And I cannot blame her totally because her son, my husband, was a willing partici-pant. After many discussions and my being upset, my husband finally made the decision to cut the ties and keep his mother out of our personal business. My advice to a wife would be to keep crit-icisms of your spouse to yourself, and encourage your husband to not share your business, personal or financial, with his mother."

Let the wise hear and increase in learning.
—Proverbs 1:5 ESV

The Holidays

Most of the daughters-in-law and mothers-in-law who responded to my questionnaire expressed the stress of dividing time between families during the holiday season. Some families lived very near their in-laws and some lived hours away, sometimes in another state. I will summarize their thoughts.

Holidays are a special time for families, especially Christmas. Some family members live almost next door to the in-laws and some live quite a distance away. It is always exciting when everyone can get together and Christmas gatherings are a priority.

Young families often feel the stress of dividing time between parents' homes. One family planned one of their vacation weeks so they could be with each set of in-laws during this time. Both sets of in-laws lived near to each other, but the young family was a long way from them. Because of space to accommodate their family, they always spent the nights with the wife's parents, who had no visitors or grands but them. Then they spent the days with the husband's family who lived only 12 miles away. They wanted the children to enjoy both families and to divide the time equally, but it rarely happened. Most waking hours were spent with the husband's family, which was quite large with many cousins. The children had fun playing in the barn, roaming the woods, and riding horses. But when it came time to return to the wife's family, comments from those in-laws caused them to feel guilty for leaving, even though her parents had no other guests.

Keep criticisms of your spouse to yourself.

Another young couple expressed the stress of being pulled between the families. While visiting one set of grandparents, calls came from the other set inquiring of their schedule. They could not even sit through a meal without getting a phone call pressuring them to hurry.

Families who live near each other all year are not immune to pressure either. A daughter told of how she rushed from one place to another: her parents, his parents, her grandparents, his grandparents, and even one great-grandparent demanding that she be at their house for Christmas dinner. Finally she said, "I think I will stay home."

Consider these issues unselfishly. As one young family so aptly expressed it, "Please be patient with us. We are trying our best to accommodate everyone, and we sometimes even dread the holiday experience because of pressures. We love you all and want our children to enjoy you. We will do our best to visit everyone. But just walk in our shoes for one season, be unselfish by sharing us, and please do not cry when we leave. We want the children to be happy and see you happy as we all wave goodbye. We will be back!"

What Shall We Do?

Some of these issues may be related to the drama issues we talked about before. And some may be related to the letting-go issue we spoke about. Parents of grown children need to give serious thought to their actions to ensure they're helping the glue in their children's families stick, rather than trying to pull them apart by not letting go. Remember what God said in Genesis 2:24 and emphasized again in Ephesians 5:31, that a man is to leave his father and mother and cleave to his wife, and they are to be one flesh. Parents, let them leave.

Mothers-in-law and daughters-in-law, pay attention: Stop the drama and just love each other.

> When faced with senseless drama, spiteful criticisms, and misguided opinions, walking away is the best way to stand up for yourself. To respond with anger is an endorsement of their attitude![3]

As my "no-drama mama" said, "The more you stir a cow pile, the worse it smells." Or the more recent phrase from the movie *Frozen*: "Let it go, let it go." So let's stop the drama, relax, and enjoy the family. We are all different and God made us that way. We can complement each other in our differences or we can make ourselves and everyone miserable by thinking we all must act and look and think alike.

Jesus provides a simple solution: "Whatever you wish that others would do to you, do also to them" (Matthew 7:12 ESV). What a difference we would see in our relationships if we all seriously considered and worked to achieve the goal of treating others like we want them to treat us. Think on these things (Philippians 4:8)!

Cultural Differences

I have a relative who has an international family. She and her husband adopted a beautiful five-year-old girl of Dutch and Korean descent. She grew up and married a Kentucky man, and they have two little boys. Her son married a naturalized citizen from Mexico. They also have two sons. The family embraces three cultures: American, Korean, and Mexican. Each has distinct family traditions.

I observed that their family was loving and united, so I asked, "What advise will you give that will help us see more ways to get along? What are some intentional actions that make peace?"

My cousin laughed. "I learned to eat kimchee and to make peanut brittle." Then she explained further, "That's true. But it's not big things that bind us together. It's the little things."

Her daughter's natural grandmother made huge batches of delicious peanut brittle as a Christmas tradition. "I volunteered to help her," my cousin said. "Then I gradually took on more of the task, learning secrets of making the recipe successfully." Grandmother appreciated the help and was delighted that the younger woman wanted to learn from her.

Keeping connections and open communication for all sides of the family is very important. "You can't have too many people to love you," my cousin said.

Then she asked her daughter-in-law, "What did I do that made you know that I loved you and was glad you were family?"

The answer was a reminder of something long forgotten: "Remember when we were on our honeymoon and you took my mom to the grocery store to show you what products I liked? You stocked the pantry with my favorite foods."

Look for ways to be loving in your words and actions.

> The more you stir a cow pile, the worse it smells.

The bride's mother is a fabulous cook, especially of traditional Mexican dishes. Their tradition of making tamales at Christmas is another way they bind their family together. For years, the mother-in-law sent tamales to her daughter-in-law. Eventually the younger woman began helping to make the ethnic dishes and the food created a festive time of family gathered around the kitchen table, chatting and enjoying their bond of family love. It did not happen overnight.

Perhaps this closeness has not yet happened in your kitchen. Bonding is a lifelong process. Look for opportunities within your family to listen, learn, serve, and praise. Remember this admonition from Paul:

> For you are all sons of God through faith in Christ Jesus. For as many of you as were baptized into Christ have put on Christ. There is neither Jew nor Greek, there is neither slave nor free, there is neither male nor female; for you are all one in Christ Jesus (Galatians 3:26–28 NKJV).

I also interviewed a lovely southern girl who was the wife of a Spanish preacher. Her advice was much the same as that above. She concluded:

> Overcoming cultural differences in this precious relationship is not much different from same-culture differences. We all want to be loved and to love. And we all have in common the desire to please Jesus by obeying His words, "Love one another."

Pleasant words are like a honeycomb,
sweetness to the soul and health to the bones.
—Proverbs 16:24 NKJV

It's Your Turn

1. Define "boundary." What boundaries can a mother-in-law observe with sons-in-law and daughters-in-law? Name two boundaries that a daughter-in-law would most appreciate.

2. How can you as a daughter-in-law encourage friendship with your in-laws?

3. Fill in the blanks below and then list three ways to apply this "thinking" advice.

   "Whatever things are _____, whatever things are _____, whatever things are _____, whatever things are _____, whatever things are _____, whatever things are of _____, if there is any virtue and if there is anything praiseworthy, meditate on _____" (Philippians 4:8 NKJV).

Recommended Reading

The Mother-in-Law Dance by Annie Chapman

Boundaries by Drs. Henry Cloud and John Townsend

Telling Yourself the Truth by William Backus and Marie Chapian

Widows do not want to be viewed with pity, dismissed as not relevant, and hidden away in loneliness. They want to be a working part of the Lord's family, not set aside. Remember, even the strongest person can be undone under the weight of isolation, loss of physical strength, and lack of purpose. Keeping the faith is different when you are suffering physical pain and personal loss. When getting out of a chair becomes a struggle, daily tasks seem daunting. Is this not the most wonderful opportunity to bring the mentoring touch of encouragement, hope, and appreciation?

—Laura Dayton

Chapter 9

Mentor Me, I'm a Widow in Distress

by Laura Dayton

Have you ever had a feeling that you have forgotten to do something for someone but, for the life of you, you can't remember what it was? Those over sixty laughingly refer to this as a "senior moment." Such was the case recently. The conversation by text went something like this.

"Hey, my sister! Was I supposed to send you information about something? Perhaps that tea recipe? Got too much in my brain these days. LOL."

The friend's response: "That's funny, would I remember? Ha,ha."

What a pair. We can laugh now, but this is just a peek into the window of an aging body and mind. Actually the more of these "moments" we experience, the less funny they become.

One day we will all need a bit of help, maybe even a lot of help, as we try to manage the mental and physical challenges of life. What would it mean to you to have a loving sister by your side walking life's road as would a daughter or best friend? With the great distances separating today's families, it is more important than ever to fill the gap and become that special family for a widow in distress.

The death of a husband immediately puts the widow into a different world, so we need a network of friends. Join clubs and do volunteer work in the church and community. Not only will you develop friendships, but you also will have the satisfaction of helping others. Create hobbies that give you mental and physical enjoyment. "Loneliness is a second death," my mother kept quoting to us, so make sure you have outside interests to keep loneliness at bay. Hold on to this truth: when one door in life is closed, the Father will open another.

111

Keep your eye on doors that will open, rather than habitually looking back longingly at the closed door.[1]

Who Are These Women and What Do They Need to Know?

The godly Christian widow is trusting God to provide what she needs. "Now she who is really a widow and left alone, trusts in God and continues in supplications and prayers night and day" (1 Timothy 5:5 NKJV). As we think of mentoring her by coming alongside, perhaps her greatest need is for love, companionship, and someone to listen. Sadly, she is often excluded and isolated.

No matter how we plan and prepare our hearts as married women, nothing comes close to the reality of the loss of a mate. This is particularly true for older women who have enjoyed decades of married life with one spouse. If you could glance into the quiet places where widows dwell, perhaps you could hear this song:

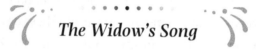

The Widow's Song

Cast upon my scene of days
A shadow enfolds my heart.
No sunrise can rejoice my steps
Nor distract griefs looming part.

Oh where's the hand that held
    me steady,
That rocked my soul to sleep?
The arms that kept me safely,
When I was brought to weep?

The laugh that was so highly gifted,
To lift me toward my goal?
The wise and caring words of truth,
To help a wounded soul?

O I will live, though you're not here,
I'll cast my cares upon God.
I will hasten to His throne,
Giving thanks, while walking
    earth's sod.

But as I step into all I do,
This one thing I know,
I will always, always, be missing
    you
As into my days I go.

How to Begin

Scripture reveals that our Lord was "a man of sorrows and acquainted with grief" (Isaiah 53). At the tomb of His dear disciple Lazarus, Jesus wept in grief along with Mary and Martha. Our heavenly Father knows the sorrows we face. James expresses what he thinks is the purest form of religion: "To visit orphans and widows in their distress" (James 1:27), the most vulnerable among us. Our measure of love and likeness to Christ can be seen in how we serve and mentor them.

We must realize that our mentoring to widows in the church is not so much a ministry of teaching and training but of mentoring hope and comfort through loving service. Are we willing to listen and learn from those who have traveled before us?

Please see the condition thrust upon these women by the loss of their mate. Put yourself in their shoes. James describes them as being in distress. What is distress? It is a state of being in pain, grief, anxiety, suffering, and trouble. It is characterized as causing anguish, which is an acute mental suffering that is often enduring and all-consuming. Is it any wonder that God left clear instruction that in practicing our Christian faith, visiting and caring for our widows is something we should take to heart?

In an article written by Betty Bender titled "Remember Us? We're Still Alive!" she reveals the plight of many widows today. Betty can speak with authority on this subject. She, along with many others in her situation, is sometimes regarded in unhelpful ways, unhelpful and far from the spirit of mentoring encouragement into their lives. They do not want to be viewed with pity, dismissed as not relevant, and hidden away in loneliness. They want to be a working part of the Lord's family, not set aside. Remember, even the strongest person can be undone under the weight of isolation, loss of physical strength, and lack of purpose.

> Well reported for good works: if she has brought up children, if she has lodged strangers, if she has washed the saints' feet, if she has relieved the afflicted, if she has diligently followed every good work (1 Timothy 5:10 NKJV).

A Woman Full of Good Works

What do you remember about Joppa? A true disciple of Christ lived there who was counted worthy of a miracle—death to life. Her name was Dorcas. We are not given much information concerning this woman of God, but what is said is highly commendable and worth imitation. Simply stated, scripture reads,

> At Joppa there was a certain disciple named Tabitha, which is translated Dorcas. This woman was full of good works and charitable deeds which she did (Acts 9:36 NKJV).

Read the following verses describing Dorcas' illness and death (Acts 9:37–43). She was greatly mourned by the widows who were richly blessed by her deeds, as evidenced by the garments she provided.

The apostle Peter entered the scene and, by the will and power of God, brought her back to life and presented her to those who loved her. Not only did this woman bless others by her deeds, but in her death and return to life, many believed in the Lord and were blessed with saving faith in the Christ. Dorcas was an example of humble service toward others, coupled with genuine love. Her character impacted the lives of many, both in life and in death. Even today, her example is one to be copied.

> Then he gave her his hand and lifted her up; and when he had called the saints and widows, he presented her alive. And it became known throughout all Joppa, and many believed on the Lord (Acts 9: 41–42 NKJV).

She Used Her Hands to Glorify God

On the back wall of a small church building in Kentucky are two giant-sized quilts. On the quilt squares are the names of those who labored to build God's church in that location. Some brethren remain, others have gone, but their memory is enshrined in the quilts. Among the commemorative artwork is the name of Ms. Edna and her husband. They were a vital part of that small but loving congregation.

Like Dorcas, Edna had a talent for sewing which she and several other ladies shared by making glorious quilts for all occasions. Losing her sight and hearing did not deter her from doing what she could to encourage others and build up the church. She was a wonderful storyteller.

Everyone, especially the children, loved her dearly. Any visit to her tidy cottage, full of well-kept treasures and memories, immediately pulled you into her open arms. With eagerness, she demanded to hear all about your life, and most especially, the work of the Lord. As you listened, she unwrapped years of wisdom. What did she ask in return? Nothing. What did she receive? Everything she needed and more, because her heart was encased in genuine love for God and others.

Her two pew shawls remain folded in the place she left them. Sometimes a chilly sister wraps them around her shoulders. The shawls are a special reminder of an older widow who truly fulfilled 2 Timothy 4:8. Mrs. Edna truly fought the good fight, finished the race, and kept the faith. I was with her moments before her passing. She patted my hand and sweetly said: "Oh honey, I'm so happy!" She then thanked me for being there, for listening as did so many.

Sisters, remember this. Keeping the faith is different when you are suffering physical pain and personal loss. When getting out of a chair becomes a struggle, daily tasks seem daunting. Is this not the most wonderful opportunity to bring the mentoring touch of encouragement, hope, and appreciation? Older widows may need rides to worship and the doctor's office. They might need meals delivered to them. But mostly they need you—loving listeners!

Mentoring Messages

- Women need to become well-acquainted with older widows before offering help. Older women are still able to do many things for themselves, so they need to be viewed with dignity and respect (Ruth 2:11–12).

- Women need to learn patience and allow more time to navigate, if dealing with walkers and wheelchairs (1 Thessalonians 5:14).

- Women need to realize how humbling it is to ask for help. Older widows need to be reassured that we are happy and blessed to serve them (Ephesians 6:5–8).

- Women need to listen with interest, seeking to find the message being shared and imitate their good example (1 Corinthians 11:1).

A Woman Who Submitted to Her Husband

The book of Genesis highlights many great women. In chapter 12 we are introduced to a very special woman: Sarah. Our knowledge of her begins as she is being called upon by God to follow her husband to unknown places so that His plan to send a Savior into the world will be accomplished. If you know a widow who has been in mission work or ministry, you have found a person who can identify with Sarah. These brave and faithful women follow their husbands with a tremendous amount of trust, especially in God.

The writer of Hebrews gives us a window into the character of Sarah:

> By faith Sarah herself also received strength to conceive seed, and she bore a child when she was past the age, because she judged Him faithful who had promised (Hebrews 11:11 NKJV).

A part of Sarah's faith was obedience to her husband. Peter states, "As Sarah obeyed Abraham, calling him lord, whose daughters you are if you do good and are not afraid with any terror" (1 Peter 3:6 NKJV).

How very much we need the example of Sarah among women today, even in the Lord's church. How many works of service and evangelism are undone because a wife is unwilling to support her husband and follow his spiritual lead. Widows who have a long history of submitting in faithfulness to their husbands need our listening ear as they teach and equip us to carry on their work in the church.

Three Mama Bears

I have already shared with you the relationship I had with Ms. Edna, a recent Mama Bear in my life. I was given two others. First, Doris Ulrick who birthed me, loved me, and taught me right from wrong. She lived what she believed earnestly. The second Mama Bear is Betty Bender who spiritually mentored me in my last forty years as a New Testament Christian. She and my mother remain great encouragers and storytellers to this day.

How can I show respect to these great women of faith? I can esteem their instruction. Widows who have seen long life generally are "bottom line" people. As did Solomon, they have come to the end of life and know well what is most important. They have suffered losses and won many victories. The greatest stress for them is the inability to enjoy the freedom to engage in busy interactions and activities they relished. It is my aim to help fill their emotional tanks and tell them how abundantly they have blessed me and helped me.

In a throwaway culture that often disrespects and disregards older women, we as God's daughters need to demonstrate His standards for widows. They know the "old paths" which are tried and true. My "Mama Bears" planted the Word deep within my heart. Perhaps they do not remember what they did yesterday or even in the last hour, but they have the sense and wisdom of God's truths ready at all times in their minds. Here is a description of their motivation:

> Diligently keep yourself, lest you forget the things your eyes have seen, and lest they depart from your heart all the days of your life. And teach them to your children and your grandchildren (Deuteronomy 4:9 NKJV).

Let us heed our mothers in the faith!

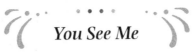

You See Me

(The following poem is dedicated to my "Mama Bears" who have seen me with the eyes of God.)

With eyes of love is our Father's gaze,
He watches us to guide our days.
The steady hope His love does bring,
Gives flight to life and makes us sing!

He sees us as we truly are,
Yet lights the sky with His morning Star.
So too are those He sends our way,
Whose eyes see us clearly in our day-to-day.
Those who tend our wounds and hear our cries,
Who lift us up when we are unwise,
Those moms of faith so rare and true,
Gifted to us because God knew
That in this life of toil and care
We would need special women to always be there.
So if you are blessed by God's great love,
With special older women directed from above,
Thank them and Him along your way,
And remember them always when you pray.

—Laura Dayton

Mentoring Messages

- Women need to realize that they will most likely be widowed. Our older sisters who are experiencing widowhood can help prepare us for such a distressful time. Remember, both Naomi and Ruth were widows. Naomi greatly helped her daughter-in-law to find a new life after a devastating loss.

- Women need to learn that obedience is the stepping stone to long life and blessings in Christ. God is faithful. Widows who have walked in the faith, like Sarah, have learned to trust God and their husbands. This trust results in far less stress and much better decisions, because they have learned how to submit to the will of God.

- Women need to be reminded that there is no leadership before followship! We must learn how to live God's way before we can teach others. I'm not referring to head knowledge, but rather to the kind of faith that comes from time and testing. Older women and widows have much to share in this regard.

Nature says you, a woman, will outlive your dear beloved husband, but your Bridegroom will never leave you. You are the only one who can separate yourself from Jesus. When you are left alone, you are a widow by earthly rules, but you will never be a widow to your Bridegroom. Then you will truly grow closer to Jesus. Widows are very special to the Father and to Jesus.[2]

It's Your Turn

1. When was the last time you had an extended conversation with an older woman? What was your takeaway from that experience?

2. How many older widows in your congregation might need a ride to worship or to appointments, or an invitation to a family meal?

3. Many widows have family members who live far away. Why not adopt a widow to be a part of your family circle? Include her in holiday parties, birthday events, and special outings. Write her name here and begin praying for mentoring opportunities.

4. If you do invite a widow over for a meal and you have young children, be aware that older women are frail and have a concern about falling. How can you teach children to conduct themselves properly around older ladies?

5. Remember, hearing loss is a real issue among older widows. Frustration is inevitable when there is a lot of background noise. If you take her to a restaurant, be sure it is relatively quiet and that you sit close enough to her that she can hear what you're saying. Nothing is more isolating than not being able to understand what others in the group are talking about. Again, patience is required because you may have to repeat what you're saying several times.

Becky Fowler Blackmon has come full circle—from Texas to New England to Georgia and back to Texas. She is well-known as a writer and a speaker, and her books, *The Begging Place, A Pearl Seeker,* and *Seek the Precious Moments* continue to top her publisher's best-seller list. She is the wife of an elder, Jeff Blackmon. They have been married for forty-eight years and have two children and five grandchildren. Becky loves cooking, antiques, and family gatherings. Her mission in this life is to help her sisters love the Lord more.

Chapter 10

Mentor Me, I'm Learning to Love My Husband

by Becky Blackmon

God was the matchmaker in the Garden of Eden. He also was the father of the bride, the father of the groom, the wedding planner, and the minister of the ceremony, all rolled into one.

It was God who brought Eve to Adam and instituted the sacred rite of marriage. Please note that God did not bring several women for Adam—just one. From the very beginning, God has ordained one man for one woman.

Let us look at this very first marriage:

> The man gave names to all the cattle, and to the birds of the sky, and to every beast of the field, but for Adam there was not found a helper suitable for him. So the Lord God caused a deep sleep to fall upon the man, and he slept; then He took one of his ribs and closed up the flesh at that place. The Lord God fashioned into a woman the rib which He had taken from the man, and brought her to the man. The man said, "This is now bone of my bones, and flesh of my flesh; She shall be called Woman, because she was taken out of Man." For this reason a man shall leave his father and his mother, and be joined to his wife; and they shall become one flesh (Genesis 2:20–24).

Do we, as women, consider verse 18, which states that God decided to make a helper, one that was suitable for Adam? Simply put, woman was made to be man's helper, not the other way around. Man was not created to be the woman's helper.

Now before we all get bent out of shape and start arguing, let's admit to the wonderful fact that in a marriage the husband and the wife both help each other. Right? A marriage is truly give-and-take, with both parties giving a hundred percent—that is the ideal. I am just trying to get across to all of us that God created woman for man and not vice versa.

Experience Teaches

Let's look at some thought-provoking words my mom had to say about marriage:

> God made the stronger first, and then, in His divine wisdom, He made the weaker, the one who would always need to be encircled. The word *husband* means the "house-binder," the encircler. Just as God made the grass before He made the beast, so He made man, then woman, and then child . . .
>
> Wouldn't you love to have seen Eve? Just imagine her beauty! Wouldn't you love to have seen Adam's face when he saw this woman, fashioned by the hands of God! What a happy day that wedding day. And what a wonderful place to spend your honeymoon!
>
> God did not give Adam a child for a companion. Children are wonderful, exciting, and fill a very needed place in our lives, but they cannot supply what is lacking in man. God did not make another man for Adam. Another man would have removed some of the loneliness, but would still not have been able to supply all the needs. Woman's very femininity, her perceptions, and her tenderness are desirable qualities to a man. We know that whatever was lacking in Adam was supplied by Eve, for God made a helper suitable for him.[1]

It is an honor and privilege to be wives, helpers to our husbands. We don't always realize this, of course, when we are first married. We think the world revolves around us personally! However, as we jump on that wild merry-go-round called "life with husband and children," we quickly grow up, or we should. And many times in the middle of this turbulent ride, we examine our role as a Christian wife and rate our progress. Sometimes we are happy with ourselves, and others times we are not.

What Is Pleasing to Him

Remember, God made women to be helpers. Our desire is to please our husbands, and we add others to that list: parents, church, brothers, and sisters. May we also never forget that loving God and being His daughters should cause us to want to please our husbands and thus please Him in the process.

A marriage is truly give-and-take, with both parties giving a hundred percent—that is the ideal.

Someone in the professional world once said that there are three stages of marriage: romance, competition, and acceptance. Yes, that describes many marriages I know, my own included.

Let me explain a bit. Most marriages start out with great passion and romantic love—the honeymoon phase. Then reality sets in with balancing jobs, finances, household duties, and rearing children. It becomes easier and easier for partners to compete with one another, seeing who can successfully maneuver these stressful responsibilities. By the way, no one wins this competition, which I call "Annie Get Your Gun": *Anything you can do, I can do better.* Finally, as children leave the nest and more time and money become available, the married couple experiences a truce of sorts. Stresses decrease, and a more enduring love often enters the picture.

I will make this statement flat out, right now: Marriage is not easy and neither is staying married. To begin with, most of us marry our opposites. How many can relate to a husband who is so attractive in the beginning but gradually becomes one who can make you pull your hair out?

The very traits of character which we find to be annoying under the stress of everyday living are usually the ones which attracted us in the first place. For example, if you are cool, composed, and always in complete control . . . you were no doubt fascinated by someone who was expressive . . . warm, and passionate. If you had always allowed money to flow through your fingers like water, you were naturally attracted to someone who possessed what you lacked—the ability to live frugally.[2]

The McWhorters continued, "Differences in marriage can be better tolerated if they can only be understood." Otherwise Satan moves into our homes, marriages suffer, and misery ensues. Sometimes love, passion, and attraction disappear. It is easier to walk away than to stay in the relationship. Our God knew this would happen. So He wisely gives us His Word to help us love and maintain good marriages. Listen to these passages:

- "Enjoy life with the woman whom you love all the days of your fleeting life which He has given to you under the sun; for this is your reward in life and in your toil in which you have labored under the sun" (Ecclesiastes 9:9).

- "Wives, be subject to your own husbands, as to the Lord. For the husband is the head of the wife, as Christ also is the head of the church, He Himself being the Savior of the body. But as the church is subject to Christ, so also the wives ought to be to their husbands in everything. Husbands, love your wives, just as Christ also loved the church and gave Himself up for her, so that He might sanctify her, having cleansed her by the washing of water with the word, that He might present to Himself the church in all her glory, having no spot or wrinkle or any such thing; but that she would be holy and blameless. So husbands ought also to love their own wives as their own bodies. He who loves his own wife loves himself; for no one ever hated his own flesh, but nourishes and cherishes it, just as Christ also does the church, because we are members of His body. For this reason a man shall leave his father and mother and shall be joined to his wife, and the two shall become one flesh" (Ephesians 5:22–31).

- "Two are better than one because they have a good return for their labor. For if either of them falls, the one will lift up his companion. But woe to the one who falls when there is not another to lift him up. Furthermore, if two lie down together they keep warm, but how can one be warm alone?

And if one can overpower him who is alone, two can resist him. A cord of three strands is not quickly torn apart" (Ecclesiastes 4:9–12).

- "Wives, be subject to your husbands, as is fitting in the Lord. Husbands, love your wives and do not be embittered against them" (Colossians 3:18–19).

How interesting that in both the passages from Ephesians and Colossians, the wife is told to be in subjection to her husband, while the husband is instructed to love his wife. Ponder that one.

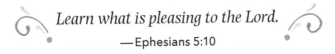

Learn what is pleasing to the Lord.
—Ephesians 5:10

Commit to God and Husband

One of my mentors, Betty Bender, told me two things about husbands. I have never forgotten her advice. She told me, "Take care of your husband." And then she added, "You have been placed here to support your husband and be there for him!"

What wonderful words of wisdom! Too many times we women are so wrapped up in ourselves and our children that we don't see our husbands, their needs, and their concerns. We just take them for granted—the very thing we accuse them of doing to us. Right, girls?

The reality and bottom line of this man-and-woman thing is that men need women, and women need men. That will never change. Now, consider something else. When we became Christians, we chose to serve God and follow Him and His commandments. And when we chose to serve God, we also chose to serve Him in our marriages. Serving the Father means serving the husbands we have, too, because being

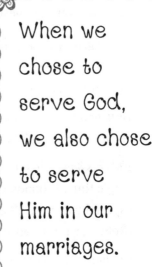

When we chose to serve God, we also chose to serve Him in our marriages.

a Christian covers every single aspect of our lives—especially our personal relationships.

> Follow the Father's compass to be the best wife. Being perfect, as Matthew 5:48 instructs us to be, is not the sinless perfection of Jesus and the Father; rather, it means to have reached the end; to have become complete, mature. It is the idea of goodness. It is a constant alertness that motivates us to continue learning God's Word, meditating upon it, and allowing its wisdom to mold us into the holiness and perfection of our Father's nature. [3]

It is in the marriage ceremony that couples vow to love one another "until death do us part." Solemn pledges and promises are made to God along with prayers for His blessings upon that sacred union. Dave Willis once wrote, "Great marriages aren't the result of luck; they're the result of commitment." It is our commitment to God that keeps us from walking away from a marriage undergoing tough times.

It takes work . . . hard work. And a whole lotta love. But most of all, my sisters, it takes God. I remember Mom telling me, "God can make any marriage a success—as long as the two people are faithful Christians."

Here are some suggestions for wives:

1. *Be a Barnabas!* Be your husband's number one fan. Encourage him over and over to seek the Lord. Encourage him in his role as a servant, husband, and father. That is the Lord's will for him.

2. *Be your husband's personal cheerleader!* Help him in his insecurities and inferiority complexes. Build him up.

3. *Hold his hand!* Hold hands when prayers are said at church services, every single time. It bonds you. It makes you forgive. It softens your heart too, especially if you walked into the church building madder than a wet hen. (Remember, it is working on him too.)

4. *Get in the Word together!* Read the Bible every day together. (My husband and I read aloud.) That will make you grow spiritually with the Lord. It will increase your faith. It will strengthen the "ties that bind" you and your

husband, and you will talk more about the Bible every day as you walk through its pages. You will count your blessings as you see how magnificently the Lord has worked in your life together.

5. *Make God happy!* Serving God means serving your husband too. Be his everything. God is first . . . then your husband.

Without a Word

Someone reading this is already asking, "Becky, what if my husband is not a believer? What if he is not a Christian? What can I do? Is there any hope for me?" To those who have this challenge, I say, "Pray. Pray. Pray. Don't give up. Pray for God to give him time; pray for God to touch his heart; pray to be strong and a good example. Beg God and put the following powerful passage into practice."

> In the same way, you wives, be submissive to your own husbands so that even if any of them are disobedient to the word, they may be won without a word by the behavior of their wives, as they observe your chaste and respectful behavior. Your adornment must not be merely external—braiding the hair, and wearing gold jewelry, or putting on dresses; but let it be the hidden person of the heart, with the imperishable quality of a gentle and quiet spirit, which is precious in the sight of God (1 Peter 3:1–4).

It takes work . . . hard work. And a whole lotta love. But most of all, my sisters, it takes God.

Do everything you can to live the Christian life 24/7 in front of your husband and children. They are watching and remembering your faith and your example.

Those of us who have Christian husbands should put 1 Peter 3:1–4 into practice. What a challenge to live Christ and show Christ without even opening our mouth! That is especially hard for me. I feel like I have to say something. But God has expressly stated: "without a word." End of discussion.

Girls, at the end of the day, we women must be women of faith. How? That's easy. We must get into the Word! And never stop. If "faith comes from hearing and hearing by the word of Christ" (Romans 10:17), then

- I need to be a good Bible student.
- I need to be a daily Bible reader.
- I need to know the difference between reading the Bible and studying the Bible.

How to Help My Husband? Don't Be a Stumbling Block.

How can I help my husband be the Christian man God wants him to be if I am not the Christian woman I need to be? If the husband is an elder, deacon, or preacher, the wife's role embraces heavy responsibilities. It is true that all Christians are servants in the Master's kingdom, but the man who chooses to serve in leadership positions certainly needs a loving Christian wife—a wife who loves God, loves the church Jesus purchased with His own blood, and loves to do her part for the Lord. After all, isn't it true that a man who wants to shepherd the flock or to serve as a deacon will never be able to do so without a dutiful wife? She is one of the keys to his even being considered to serve the congregation (1 Timothy 3:2, 4, 12). Who is going to nominate a man for one of these important, serious offices if his wife is a troublemaker, gossip, or worldly woman? It just will not happen—or should not happen.

Oh, my sisters, how careful we must be in our behavior and appearance! What wife in her right mind wants to cause reproach and derision upon her own husband? Let's take this one step further and ask, What Christian woman really desires to be a stumbling block in God's plan for her husband and his future role in the church? The church needs and will always need strong men who will lead and strong women who will recognize the importance of that leadership. It is certainly a given that we women must help God's plan—not abort it.

To the women who are reading this chapter and leading miserable troubled lives due to a stubborn, silent, non-communicative husband, please hear me out. Remember, the Lord can fix anything, but first, my sisters, you must beg God for help. Go to the begging place and pour out your heart before the throne of God. Read the story of Hannah in 1 Samuel and see how she poured out her heart "before the Lord."

Jesus, our wonderful High Priest, will intercede for you as He has promised:

> Therefore, since we have a great high priest who has passed through the heavens, Jesus the Son of God, let us hold fast our confession. For we do not have a high priest who cannot sympathize with our weaknesses, but One who has been tempted in all things as we are, yet without sin.

Therefore let us draw near with confidence to the throne of grace, so that we may receive mercy and find grace to help in time of need (Hebrews 4:14–16).

How can I help my husband be the Christian man God wants him to be if I am not the Christian woman I need to be?

Pray to the heavenly Father to help, to do, and to fix. Pray for Jesus, your heavenly bridegroom, to repair your earthly bridegroom.

Next, I encourage you to do everything you can to get professional help. Your marriage is at stake, and there are marriage counselors who can perhaps help to turn your marriage around. Most are skilled, educated, and very understanding when it comes to broken relationships. I implore you: please, please get help.

God, in His marvelous mercy and wisdom, has given us the ideal woman to emulate in Proverbs 31:10–31. We call her the Worthy Woman, and she reigns as our role model. Remember our admiration for her? Let's see how God describes her:

An excellent wife, who can find?
For her worth is far above jewels.
The heart of her husband trusts in her,
And he will have no lack of gain.
She does him good and not evil
All the days of her life (vv. 10–12).

Read the rest of Proverbs 31 from your own Bible. Say your own name, rather than "she." God is giving you a pattern.

Woman Impossible

In Proverbs 31, God issues one of the greatest challenges a Christian woman can face. What woman can read that passage and not feel inadequate, imperfect, and somewhat exhausted? All of us have trouble with Proverbs 31. But we must remember that God gave us these words to help us, not hurt us. These verses describe the woman who loves God and then loves her husband and family. The worthy woman fears God and has great respect for Him and for His Word.

Where do we fit in, my sister? Is it impossible to be like the Worthy Woman? I say no! If my Savior said "with God all things are possible" (Matthew 19:26), then I certainly know that I can become like her! The challenge before all of us women is whether or not we want to be like her. Will we choose to be like her?

I once asked my husband, "Why do you love me?" I always ask him questions like that. Jeff is not a verbal man, but when he needs to come through, man, he comes through! So he answered my question: "Because you are good for me." I translate that into being his helper. Don't we all want to be good for one another in this lifelong commitment we have made?

I saw a post on Trey Morgan's Facebook page about an ordinary day with him and his wife Lea.

> My wife has brought me coffee today, told me that I was awesome, and fixed me supper. She loves me.
>
> I've let her sleep in, reminded her that she's beautiful, and filled her car up with gas. I love her.

MENTOR ME, I'M LEARNING TO LOVE MY HUSBAND

Marriage is about the little things. It's as good as two people are willing to make it.

Marriage isn't always what you may think or hear . . . it's better.

There is a phrase going around, and perhaps you have heard it too. It goes like this: "Happy wife, happy life!" It means that in a marriage, it is the wife who must be catered to. Keeping her happy is of the utmost importance. I must admit, I like it when the marriage revolves around me.

But let us do some "God thinking" about marriage, this marvelous institution the Lord has given us. What would happen to marriages everywhere if we changed that saying to "Happy hubby and wife, happy life"?

It's Your Turn

1. Is it always easy to be the wife—the helper God wants the woman to be in a marriage? Why or why not?

2. List ways a wife can be a stumbling block when her husband is considering becoming a deacon, elder, or preacher.

3. How can a wife be an asset if her husband is considering becoming a deacon, elder, or preacher?

4. What does it take to make a good godly marriage?

5. For those of you who have been married awhile, give examples of important lessons God has taught you in your marriage.

6. Read the Song of Solomon.

Once we are convinced of our debt to God for our salvation, the opportunities for teaching will arise and motivate us to dig more deeply in God's Word. We want to know God!. When you keep putting the Word in your mind, it will find its way out. Simply put, you just can't stop talking about the Lord because He is on your mind all day long. Paul knew this feeling well and expressed it this way, "For if I preach the gospel, I have nothing to boast of, for I am under compulsion; for woe is me if I do not preach the gospel" (1 Corinthians 9:16).

—Becky Blackmon

Chapter 11

Mentor Me, I'm Learning to Teach

by Becky Blackmon

The scene is set before us. The place: Jerusalem. The event: the crucifixion of the Son of God. The exact spot: Calvary. The date: circa AD 30–33.

> There were also women looking on from afar, among whom were Mary Magdalene, Mary the mother of James the Less and of Joses, and Salome, who also followed Him and ministered to Him when He was in Galilee, and many other women who came up with Him to Jerusalem (Mark 15:40–41 NKJV).

There they were. There they stood for hours. Never leaving. Who were these women? Women who understood who Jesus really was. Women who wanted to help the Messiah. Women who wanted to follow Him wherever He went—even to the cross. Women who needed a Savior. Women just like us.

It is interesting to note that all four gospel accounts of Christ's life mention the presence of the women at the cross (Matthew 27:55; Mark 15:40–41; Luke 23:49; John 19:25).

James Burton Coffman, my favorite commentary writer, had this to say about these women:

> The gospels present women as the spiritual leaders of the race. They were last with Jesus at the cross, first to behold his resurrection, and everywhere more perceptive than men. It was a woman that won the city of Sychar for Jesus, a woman that anointed him for burial; and here Mark recounts a multitude that followed him from Galilee. Thank God for women, without whose spiritual perception and fidelity the race of man would indeed be almost helpless. Blessed are their names which are written in the book of life.[1]

Luke tells us that these women even helped to support these men out of their own pocketbooks.

> Soon afterwards, He began going around from one city and village to another, proclaiming and preaching the kingdom of God. The twelve were with Him, and also some women who had been healed of evil spirits and sicknesses: Mary who was called Magdalene, from whom seven demons had gone out, and Joanna the wife of Chuza, Herod's steward, and Susanna, and many others who were contributing to their support out of their private means (Luke 8:1–3).

It is not hard for us women to imagine the scene at Calvary. Neither is it difficult for us to visualize the women who walked with the Lord, caring for Him and His apostles. What a daunting task it must have been to take care of others, to travel to different cities, and to furnish all the necessities daily. How mind boggling! Just planning a one-week camping trip is enough to drive anyone crazy today. Decisions had to be made daily about the provisions for such a group, and these women saw the huge scope of what was needed to keep Jesus doing what He did best: teaching and healing and changing lives. More importantly, these women understood who Jesus really was—the Son of God. Even His apostles had trouble understanding this. But the women did not.

What Can I Do?

This passage in Luke 8 shows great love on the women's part. Love for the Lord. Love for His message. All they wanted to do was help the Lord, so they gave what they had. And that was everything, wasn't it? They evidently walked many a mile, from "one city and village to another," to follow Jesus. They gave from their own private bank account. Why would anyone do that? Because they got the picture. Because they saw a Savior and they saw salvation. These women gave what they had and did what they could for Jesus.

We totally comprehend the scene in Luke 10 where Martha has invited a group of hungry men to her home for a meal. Surrounded by all the details of getting the food on the table, Martha told Jesus to tell Mary to get up and help her. Where else in Scripture does a woman order Jesus to do something? I always chuckle at this scene. All those with an older sister chuckle, I think.

Where is Mary? Seated at the Master's feet. Listening, learning—that's Mary. What did Martha really want? To be where Mary was.

> We women understand the scene and the vexed nature of Martha, needing Mary's right hand to help prepare food for at least twelve hungry men. But we also understand Mary's longing to sit and listen to the profound teaching of the Savior. How did Jesus honor Mary on this occasion? He said, "She has chosen the good part."[2]

Why do we understand this picture God gives us of two women who wanted to serve the Lord and listen to Him too? Because that is our story today.

Why Teach?

When we realize the depth of God's love in sending Jesus to save our souls, we too want to help. We feel the need to do something! Our response to the cross should always be, "What can I do in return for Your gift, my Father?" When we honestly fathom the gift of salvation so freely given to all and the multitude of our own sins, our hearts are deeply touched to respond.

God knew this would happen, and one of the biggest blessings of our lives is that our Father placed us in the church that belongs to His Son. "And the Lord was adding to their number [the church] day by day those who were being saved" (Acts 2:47).

There is much work to be done in the family of God. We learn about sacrifice and forgiveness too. We learn to grow up and flourish as God's

They gave what they had. And that was everything.

child. That is why being faithful to attend the services is so important. If we are absent from worship, we miss out on the many opportunities provided there to learn and grow spiritually. And how can we please God if we have not gathered with our church family to serve others, help spread the Gospel, and tell what the Lord has done for us?

A Place for the Saved

The sisterhood begins in the church. The Lord has brought us together, and that is no accident. It's all a part of a bigger plan He designed for all His children. The church is our family. That is where we belong. Here we begin friendships that will take us into eternity. As women, we gravitate toward one another, taking note of those with whom we connect and those we do not. As we grow and mature in the faith, we learn to be sensitive to other women, to reach out, to care for another, to help, and to encourage. These are some of the blessings of being "in Christ."

Here is an interesting passage to note:

> These all with one mind were continually devoting themselves to prayer, along with the women, and Mary the mother of Jesus, and with His brothers (Acts 1:14).

This event happened after the ascension of Jesus. The inner circle had stayed in Jerusalem as Christ had told them to do. What were they busy doing? Were they on vacation? Were they leisurely spending their time there? No, they were not. We see the remaining apostles *and the women* were busy praying—being devoted to prayer constantly.

We are not told who the women were, but surely those same women who followed the Master continually were the ones here. Luke tells us that Jesus' mother Mary was also gathered with this assembly of saints. She was still there, praying with the others and continuing with the work ahead of her. After this, she is not mentioned again.

Go Ye Means Go Me

Not only were the women in Acts 1 praying constantly, but they were also preparing for the coming days. Peter stood among them and taught. Then a new apostle was appointed to take Judas' place. Unlike the worship days of the Old Testament, the women were right there, listening and learning and witnessing the events. New days were dawning when the women grew to understand that the command of their Savior to "go and teach and make disciples" applied to them. And that command is still ours today.

Take time to study the outstanding women in the New Testament. Phoebe, in Romans 16, is called a worker and a servant. Then there is Priscilla, an evangelistic helper (Acts 18). Philippians 4 tells of two women, Euodia and Syntyche, who had been workers with Paul, but at some point they began causing a rift in the congregation in Philippi.

Study and dig and learn all you can about these women. Then plan to become a woman who teaches "as you go." When you keep putting God's Word in your mind, it will find its way out. Simply put, you just can't stop talking about the Lord because He is on your mind all day long. Paul knew this feeling well and expressed it this way, "For if I preach the gospel, I have nothing to boast of, for I am under compulsion; for woe is me if I do not preach the gospel" (1 Corinthians 9:16). Don't put off learning or teaching. "Why the urgency?" you may ask.

> We may have a stroke and be unable to walk or talk; we may have a bout with cancer and become bedridden; our mind may begin to slip. and we lose the memory of God's Word; and with that loss of memory, gone forever are all the things we meant to do for God and with God. Then we no longer have the excuse of "I'll do it someday." Gone are the opportunities to travel to lectureships and learn and grow. Gone are the plans to attend a Tuesday morning ladies' Bible class and pray with the sisters. Gone is the mind that once knew all the books of the Bible backward and forward. . . These are gone because we have selfishly chosen shopping, sports, and events over God.[3]

I'm not covering all the nuts and bolts of teaching—just a few aspects of it. However this is certainly true: Once we are convinced of our debt to God for our salvation, and we begin to study and learn all we can, the opportunities for teaching will arise and motivate us to dig even more deeply in God's Word. We want to know God! Why do you think this work begins in our Christian life? Perhaps it is because we now understand something of what God has done for us and the debt we owe Jesus. Perhaps it is also because our Father knows the genuineness of our faith and our desire to now "go and tell it on the mountain." Either way, our life for the Lord has truly begun, and we must not look back.

Teach children, teach women, teach those who don't know the gospel. But do not put it off. Begin today. You and I will never know this side of heaven whose lives we touched. So we must keep on working for the Lord and doing our part. As my sweet mama used to say, "What a tragedy it would be to walk into heaven alone!"

Be Thankful for Women

In addition to the common truth that men need women and vice versa, as we mentioned in the previous chapter, let's also consider that women need women. We do lunch; we talk and text continually, sharing news and info all the day long. Why? This is all God's idea. He has made us very social and talkative. Women are extremely sensitive. We listen better and communicate better than men. It has been proven that girl babies talk before boy babies. That's no surprise for us, is it?

The world has always said, "Laugh and the world laughs with you, cry and you cry alone." But we women say, "Laugh and the world laughs with you, cry and you cry with your girlfriends."

Our friendships begin and oh, the women that God sends our way. We thank God for them and we pray for them. "There is a friend who sticks closer than a brother" (Proverbs 18:24). Well, it certainly is true that there is a friend who sticks closer than a sister—a soul sister.

However, we must always be on our toes as Christian women and not cause division or conflict by sharp or hurtful words. Satan thrives on that. Oh, how he loves to spark arguments and dissension between sisters. Look at James 3 and study this amazing chapter that addresses the dangers of the tongue, jealousy, and selfish ambition.

In Titus 2, God instructs older women to help teach the younger women. That makes sense. The older woman has experienced so much more than the younger woman and can easily help to soothe troubled hearts with husbands and children and relationships in the church too.

When I was grieving the loss of my own mom several years ago, a dear sister in Georgia named Tressie took me under her wing and loved me like a daughter. She came to me and said, "Becky, I will be your mama now." I cannot tell you what her words meant to me that day. I became her child and she became my mama. I needed her so.

I truly believe that God brings women into our lives to teach, to help, to befriend, and to love. I am so thankful to my Father for the women He has brought into my life. I will forever be indebted to Him and them.

There is one outstanding item to note as we close this chapter. The women who followed Jesus in Palestine and Judea so many centuries ago never left Him—never. They took care of Him until the very end of His life. They were last at the cross and first at the tomb. The question that each woman must ask herself is, *Would I have been there too?*

It's Your Turn

1. What should be our response to Jesus' sacrifice?

2. The last time the Scripture refers to Mary, the mother of Jesus, where is she and what is she doing?

3. Research and list a resource to help with teacher training in these areas: the lost, children, women, teens, adults.

4. List three excuses you have heard for not teaching. Is there a real reason for not teaching anyone?

5. Why do you think women need one another?

6. Name some women God has sent to you to teach. Then name some women who have personally taught you. What one event do you remember best? Why?

Sometimes both caregiver and "care-getter" might feel isolated and forgotten. It is easy for them to quickly detach from the world around them and become engulfed in the endless duties that soon become their world. Even that last trip to the grocery store seems to be a far-away memory. A week might feel like a month and they lose track of the days. Help is needed for their burdens. Let's carry some of their heavy load and support them in their trial.

~Laura Dayton

Chapter 12

Mentor Me, I'm a Caregiver

by Laura Dayton

Most women are caregivers. Cuts, bruises, diaper rash, coughs—whatever! Mama has to make them go away. But as the caregiver begins to experience an empty nest, her patients begin to change. Now they become mother, father, spouse, friend, or maybe even a grown child. Her task becomes very challenging indeed. If you are about to begin providing care for a physically or emotionally needy person, you are facing some major changes. How you deal with the situation makes all the difference in your ability not to "go down with the ship."

Recently, I have begun to wear the title *caregiver.* I'm often advised: "Do take care of yourself." In general, that is good advice, but what are the particulars? How exactly does the caregiver take care of herself while caring for those who cannot fully care for themselves?

On a return flight after visiting my daughter, I sat next to a very interesting older woman—a professional counselor. We talked about difficulties encountered when circumstances change, and one is suddenly thrown into the role of decision maker or caregiver. I asked her, "What exactly does a caregiver do to take care of herself? Her answer was profoundly simple: Keep your spiritual life healthy.

What daily steps can make your spiritual life healthier?

- *Remember your body.* Get enough sleep. Eat healthy and get out in the fresh air for a bit (1 Corinthians 6:19).

- *Preserve your social and spiritual contacts.* Spend time with people who lift you up and help you laugh and see life in a positive way (Proverbs 15:13; Hebrews 10:25).

- *Protect your joy.* The joy of the Lord is your strength—by the minute, by the hour, by the day (Nehemiah 8:10).

Do you want to encourage a caregiver? Paul provides a helpful guidepost in Galatians 6:2,5 for uplifting and encouraging those who need constant care. Although Paul is addressing the idea of helping one who is overtaken in a sin, it is not a stretch of context to include the concept of being overtaken in any life-altering situation. The instruction for us as Christians is to "bear one another's burdens, and thereby fulfill the law of Christ." The Greek work for *burden* is *baros,* which means "weight," implying a load or a force that is pressing heavily. When we help someone carry a heavy load, we fulfill the royal law of Christ by loving them and supporting them in their trial.

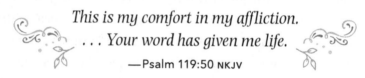

This is my comfort in my affliction.
. . . Your word has given me life.
—Psalm 119:50 NKJV

Practicalities for Final Decisions

The following advice comes from the voice of experience—one who has been through the trials of final separation from one held dear.

> The way of love is to prepare for death's separation. Start preparing now, because death comes to every age. Even if you are young and have small children, make plans in the event that you or your husband becomes a victim to accident or illness.
>
> Keep your affairs in order as best you can. Have an accessible place to keep your important papers. Know the laws of your state. Sometimes lock boxes are sealed at death until the court allows them opened, and the mate is unable to withdraw cash from the bank account. Secure your lock box and your bank accounts with both signatures, along with the signature of a trusted friend. Keep your life insurance current.

Make funeral plans. Pre-planning lifts a great burden from the bereaved at a time when many have difficulty thinking clearly. Secure a burial plot. Little things left undone add up to a big problem when the final hour comes. Both of you need to make wills even if you don't own a cent.

You cannot will your children, but you can request the court to honor your desires for the caretakers of them. Incorporate details in your will to make life easier for your mate. That means you need legal aid to help you determine things you would not think about, such as not having to make bond to settle the estate. A lawyer will save money in the long run. If you don't have a will, the state will make all the decisions for you, and those decisions will not be to the benefit of your family . . . know where the deeds and stock papers are, know a good CPA, and know a trusted lawyer.[1]

 With all lowliness and gentleness, with longsuffering, bearing with one another in love.
—Ephesians 4:2 NKJV

Don't Stop Reaching Out

Sometimes both caregiver and "care-getter" might feel isolated and forgotten. It is easy for them to quickly detach from the world around them and become engulfed in the endless duties that soon become their world. Even that last trip to the grocery store seems to be a far-away memory. A week might feel like a month and they lose track of the days.

How are we responding to their needs? One chapter of the book, *Side by Side*, is titled "When Abnormal Becomes Normal." Take note of the author's thoughts:

> Have we hardened our hearts to the suffering around us?

We are great at taking care of those in need, or are we? I think the answer to that question is yes and no. We are great on the front end. When a new crisis arises, we are Johnny-on-the-spot. However, how many of us (myself included) can write down all the names on the shut-in list? How many times have we visited or helped someone whose needs are long-term or unchanging? I'm not trying to make us feel bad. I just want us to think. Right now in your group, take a moment to see who can name every person on the long-term sick and shut-in list. I know you have one. All churches do. Sadly, these are the forgotten folks among us. Why? Their abnormal has become normal.

When they first began to struggle, it's likely that there was a lot of support, but now we have become used to their absence. Did we stop looking for them? Did we stop missing them? Did we stop reaching out to them? Probably.

Is it possible that we have become overwhelmed with the needs of the long-term sufferers? Could it be that for all of our quoting of "let us not grow weary while doing good" (Galatians 6:9) that we become weary? Or worse, is it possible that we have hardened our hearts to the suffering around us without even realizing it?[2]

Reaching out works both ways. The caregiver can reach out *for* help and we can reach out *to* help. Why don't they ask for assistance? Maybe they fear rejection or they don't want to bother others. Maybe they think, "It's easier to just do it myself." Maybe they are crying out to God, "Have mercy on me, O Lord, for I *am* weak; O Lord, heal me, for my bones are troubled" (Psalm 6:2 NKJV).

> Reaching out works both ways. The caregiver can reach out *for* help and we can reach out *to* help.

If you are a caregiver, please ask for help. Let's say a man has a debilitating stroke and his wife is suddenly bombarded with decisions. Should she order a hospital bed and take him home? Should she place him in a temporary rehab facility? Should she "go over his head" with other financial and health decisions?

Often, godly women are troubled about the delicacy of being in submission and yet being forced to override a husband's choices when he is obviously impaired due to physical trauma or a disease such as dementia or Alzheimer's.

So what is a Christian woman to do when her spiritual head, the one she has trusted in and leaned on for forty-plus years, becomes infatuated with TV's "Reverend Jones" who constantly begs for money? He can still write a check and address an envelope. And she watches as he seals it, attaches the stamp, and shuffles to the mailbox with it. Her dearest friend and hero is behaving like a deranged man, wasting family resources by encouraging a spiritual quack.

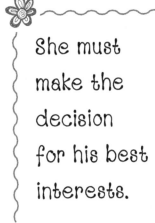

She must make the decision for his best interests.

Or perhaps he looks at her innocently one evening and makes this proposition, "If we're going to keep living together like this, don't you think we should get married?"

What is the wife's response to this type of behavior? After all, Paul says, "Wives, be subject to your own husbands, as to the Lord. For the husband is the head of the wife, as Christ also is the head of the church . . . But as the church is subject to Christ, so also the wives ought to be to their husbands in everything" (Ephesians 5:22–24). Even though she has not always agreed with her husband's decisions, she has always stood beside him and helped him to reach his goals. But the Holy Spirit never intended that His instructions regarding submission be abused by circumstances.

> *You make the decision always to act in the best interest of your husband.*
> —Patsy Loden

Should a woman say, "Well, he's head of the house. I must let him do as he wishes"? We all know better. Whatever it takes, a wise wife has to stop such irrational actions.

So make the spiritual application. When the dear man who has served so long as head of the family begins to squander family resources on unrighteous causes or begs to get married when he's already celebrated fifty years of marriage with her, his Christian wife has not only the right but also the obligation to prevent him from doing so. She should do it kindly and gently, but she must do it. If loving and general discussions do not work, she must make the decision for his best interests, even if she removes a check from the mailbox or ignores a marriage proposal.

Open your mouth for the mute, for the rights of all the unfortunate.
—Proverbs 31:8

Maybe you are standing outside the "abnormal," wondering, "What should I do first?" It can be overwhelming to become aware of needs formerly ignored. Or perhaps you are swallowed up in the abnormal world of caregiving. Both situations call for action. Once you become aware of a long-term need, look for ways to get your sisters involved. No one should be left in a position to suffer burnout, either in caregiving or in aiding a caregiver. Also, do some research as to community services or government services that might be helpful. Ask for prayer. Ask for advice from trusted Christian friends.

The bottom line: It's a battle. We sometimes sing, "The Battle Belongs to the Lord." Does it? Or are we fighting the battle all alone? Another song advises, "Ask the Savior to help you, comfort, strengthen, and keep you." Sing those songs often, whether you are caregiving or helping the caregiver. You are not alone.

Therefore humble yourselves under the mighty hand of God, that He may exalt you in due time, casting all your care upon Him, for He cares for you.
—1 Peter 5:6–7 NKJV

It's Your Turn

1. How could you help relieve others of their duties so they might worship God or attend a class?

2. Why should you be willing to take a meal to a caregiver and her family? How might your kind act lift her burden?

3. Would you be willing to visit and bring laughter and joy into a caregiver's day? Why is that important?

4. How can you encourage caregivers and let them know that God knows their needs?

5. How can you help them see the joy of the Lord that they might find strength to face the day?

And even when I am old and gray, O God, do not forsake me, until I declare Your strength to this generation, Your power to all who are to come. For Your righteousness, O God, reaches to the heavens, You who have done great things; O God, who is like You?

—David (Psalm 71:18–19)

Even to your old age I will be the same, and even to your graying years I will bear you! I have done it, and I will carry you; and I will bear you and I will deliver you.

—God (Isaiah 46:4)

Chapter 13

Mentor Me, I'm Aging

(Mentoring to the End)

Includes contributions from each author

The Final Showdown
by Becky Blackmon

Therefore we do not lose heart, but though our outer man is decaying, yet our inner man is being renewed day by day.
—2 Corinthians 4:16

Someone has once said, "Growing old is a privilege denied to many." How true! As we ride this roller coaster called life, we experience innumerable joys, sorrows, sunrises, and sunsets. Suddenly, we gaze in the mirror and see our mother's face, or we hear her voice coming out of our own mouths. Yes, we have grown old, and we don't even remember it happening.

Growing old is not a bad thing. In fact, it has its perks. We can be forgetful, and it is overlooked. We can do crazy unusual things and wear horrible outfits, and people will forgive easily. Our world looks at us and says, "Oh, she's just getting old." Now, that's a good thing.

It is imperative as Christians that we realize that our service to God has no end. We want to wear out, not rust out. Just because we have aches and pains, that does not mean we cannot still encourage one another, love one another, and tell others the good news that Jesus has come and died for them. As long as there is breath in our bodies, our work for Him goes on.

Listen to the psalmist.

> The righteous man will flourish like the palm tree,
> He will grow like a cedar in Lebanon.
> Planted in the house of the Lord,
> They will flourish in the courts of our God.
> They will still yield fruit in old age;
> They shall be full of sap and very green,
> To declare that the Lord is upright;
> He is my rock, and there is no unrighteousness in Him.
>
> —Psalm 92:12–15

As daughters of the King, we have been planted in the house of the Lord, so let us bloom there all the days of our lives. Let's flourish, yield fruit, and be young—for there is much for us still to learn. I thank God for these precious and encouraging words from this psalm, don't you?

My mom used to say to me, "Becky, you don't think you are going to get old, but you are." You were right, Mom. It has happened to me. God has let me live this long, and I rejoice that I still can get around and "do," for there are many who cannot. My dad once said to me when he was in his eighties, "Being able to breathe and walk—these are small victories!"

Take Stress Away—Write It Down

Several suggestions occur to me about age and its final showdown. There is one aspect that we must consider and boldly grasp, and that is the subject of our own death. We will die, unless the Lord comes first. Girls, what a wonderful idea it is to prepare for our death ahead of time. My parents wisely wrote out their funeral services, including the songs they wanted sung. They wrote down what pieces of furniture and beloved items were to go to which child, admonishing us never to fight or argue about perishable things. To make things easier on us kids, they went to the cemetery office and bought their plots and chose their headstones years before they departed. They sometimes even visited themselves! Their headstones were flat, had their names and decorations on them, and had only their birth dates on them, of course. They loved to go and look at their "spots" and enjoyed taking family and friends to their next "home."

> I did not have to decide on burials when my heart was broken in grief.

I cannot even begin to describe how much stress they took from me by making those decisions and selections ahead of time. I did not have to decide on their funerals, bank accounts, or burials when my heart was broken in grief. My parents were having the last "say," even though they were no longer on this earth.

There is one more thing Mom did as I was growing up that gave me peace in the last years of her life. She told me several times, "Becky, if it ever comes to the point that I can no longer take care of myself, please put me in a nursing home." She was trying to spare me that very hard decision. And yes, I did have to make that decision for her in her last year. What a sharp contrast this was with others who have said, "Do not *ever* put me in a nursing home!" Mom knew that I had to have peace, and I will always love and honor her for that.

It is not always easy to think about our last days. But death is a part of life, and it is critical to have that all-important conversation with our loved ones. May we never leave our children with the troubling question, "What would Mom want us to do?" Let's be wise women. Tell them now—before it is too late.

Facing the Final Years
by Brenda Birckholtz

 Do not cast me off in the time of old age; do not forsake me when my strength fails.
—Psalm 71:9

"Grow old along with me, the best is yet to be" is part of a poem by Robert Browning that was meant for couples, but easily applies to individuals. How can we help aging individuals to experience "the best is yet to be" part? We need to assure them, "With the Lord you don't become old, you become whole."

Besides watching the aging be challenged by diminished hearing, sight, and speech, I've noticed that some psychological/social needs painfully go unmet.

Listed below are typical statements that will fit in the category, "What You Want to Know from an Aging Person." And most likely the "aging gracefully" person will not be saying to you, "I need help." What can you hear that she is *not* saying?

1. The calls don't come in from those who formerly sought my advice.

2. I'm not asked to teach classes, speak at ladies' days, or help organize programs as I once was.

3. Although it's not intentional, I'm not included in the everyday happenings in life, probably because I don't have the faculties to respond as I once did. I'm the uninformed one, whereas I used to be the "go to" person for details.

4. As I try to cope with these losses, will you help me, please?

Our response to that last question from our aging friends should be, Yes, we will!

1. We will consciously make an effort to consistently call you, just to keep in touch. After all, you made plenty of time to keep in touch with us.

2. We will give advanced thought to an area where we need advice and ask you to give it.

3. We will help you stay involved with Bible study where you were once the teacher by:
   a. Taking you to classes.
   b. Having Bible studies with you on the phone if you wish.
   c. Making it a point to bring you outlines, bulletins, or any other material from assemblies, classes, or events.

4. To help you stay connected we will keep you informed on what's happening in the lives of people we have in common or the brotherhood in general. For example, sometimes before I call Betty, one of the co-authors of this book, I check with someone on the Board of Directors at the Christian camp in Maine to get updates on building projects, ladies' and men's retreats, etc. This means a lot to her. I check websites to see who is speaking at ladies' days/retreats throughout the Northeast and give her details. She really looks forward to this information.

In essence we can do "prep" work before calling a sweet sister or bother to help ease the pain of their social losses.

Let's determine now to truly befriend our gracefully aging friends. Most likely if you are reading this book, you are already prompted to awareness, along with action to help them. Perhaps they are not as old as you are. Or perhaps they are older. Regardless, let's not cast them away. Let's show them honor and respect, thereby showing reverence to God.

> You shall stand up before the gray head and honor the face of an old man, and you shall fear your God: I am the Lord (Leviticus 19:32 ESV).

Living in the Twilight Years Gracefully
by Martha Coletta

Her name was Cindy. We met her after worship one Sunday when the preacher invited Frank and me to walk with him across the street to the assisted living/nursing unit. "You gotta meet Cindy before you go back to New York," he said. He assured us we would never forget Cindy. Forty years have passed, and we never have.

Cindy was a member of the church, mother of one of the elders, and now living a totally dependent life. We entered her room—no decorations, no extra furnishings; just a monitor which we learned was turned on so she could hear the Bible lessons on Sundays and Wednesdays. Cindy was lying partly on her side in a crib-like bed with bars all around. She was propped by pillows, hand extended to greet us. We had been schooled to only touch her hand, not shake it or squeeze it in any way. Cindy was a victim of rheumatoid arthritis, so very crippling that a handshake could break bones. But that was not what impressed us the most.

> She's not defined by her "new normal." She has chosen to define it.

After introductions Cindy took the lead in conversing about the lesson with the preacher. She even told a funny story that complemented his lesson points. When she rehearsed the shepherd's prayer from that day and then asked who else she could pray for, I knew I had met a very special elderly woman. Cindy was a prayer warrior. Her ministry? Prayer for all the saints. And I have an idea that her prayer life was nurtured even before she became bedridden.

If you are reading this, you probably are in the club called "Growing Older." Membership is not an option. The only qualification: being blessed to live another day. So how do I grow old gracefully and remain a blessing to others? How do I continue to be pleasing to the Lord and bring honor to Him? I think Cindy found the secret for herself: focused, informed prayer for others. This worked for Cindy and brought her joy in spite of her circumstances. What a model it proved for Frank and me!

A New Normal

We have known others who have walked gracefully in their twilight years. One who stands out to me is Betty Bender, a co-author of this book. Betty lives alone at an assisted living center. Her car keys were retired several years ago; she depends on others for transportation. Yet she does not consider that a great trial; she instead invites women in twice a week for prayer and study. Those times have become very special love circles in her new home. She has reserved meeting rooms and hosted dinner for friends in private dining areas of the center. While she doesn't do the cooking anymore, she makes her guests feel right at home. She's not defined by her "new normal." She has chosen to define it.

One of Betty's talents has been the gift of writing. She had several Christian books for women published over the years. In these, her twilight years, she continues to write, often expressing a humorous story that is "oh so Betty!"

> The righteous man will flourish like the palm tree. He will grow like a cedar in Lebanon. Planted in the house of the Lord, they will flourish in the courts of our God. They will still yield fruit in old age; they shall be full of sap and very green (Psalm 92:12–14).

Betty uses her phone to update her prayer ministry. It is a comfort and a joy to know that she cares not only for her family but also wants to know how to pray for mine. She still yields "fruit in old age." What a model she extends to me.

If you are with Betty for a little while, you might hear her say, "I can't wait to go to heaven!" She's not complaining. She's smiling. She loves the Lord and longs for that day she will see Him face to face. What a reminder this is to me to reassure our grown children and grandchildren that I too long to be with the Lord, that I am not afraid of passing on, that I will be waiting for them on the other side. We who have obeyed the gospel of Jesus can claim that hope.

Statistics here in the United States report that we are all hanging around longer. While circumstances and health issues might make physical changes, our lives as disciples of Christ should grow sweeter as the days go by. The accounts of Cindy and Betty show two completely different situations of how elderly years can look. Yet they both found ways to serve, to continue to be plugged in to the Lord's concerns, to be blessings. They chose to live this verse: "Do not merely look out for your own personal interests, but also for the interests of others" (Philippians 2:4).

Discipleship does not end with old age. In fact, it's even more important. Ask Cindy, she will tell you. Observe Betty, she will show you. How precious it will be when we meet in heaven!

A Promise of Compassion and Everlasting Love
by Judy Cofer

Soon I will be seventy-six. What? Seventy-six? Is that old? I once thought so but now it does not feel old. Why, only yesterday I was twenty-one and rocking two precious little boys. Then at twenty-four, another precious baby boy was added in my arms.

Suddenly, my arms were empty of babies. Those babies were grown men with lovely wives, and my arms began to fill again—with grandchildren. What a joy! Just as quickly, the grandchildren grew up, the oldest graduating college and beginning her own fast journey to growing older. The other six are not far behind.

How am I supposed to feel at seventy-six, a place I have never been before? What am I supposed to do with these empty arms and this quiet house? What do I look like to others? In my mind's eye I still look much like I did in my forties and fifties. Then I look in the mirror and ask, "Who are you? Where did you get that gray hair and those wrinkles? They were not there last night."

Young people see me aging more than I do. Some seem to think my usefulness is gone. I accept that it is time for them to do most of the activities I used to do. But I still want to be active, especially in teaching the young. I believe I still have something to offer. The Lord has used life's happenings to teach me a plurality of lessons. I would gladly share my wisdom, but only if you ask.

My physical abilities are limited now. I recently had a bad fall because I fainted. Since then, my children, and especially my husband, have been so attentive. They are thoughtful to watch and help. And I am thankful for their assistance.

Even the youngest grandson, Hutson, got in on the "Nana watch." Recently, he and his sisters, Crismon and Anna Kate, were visiting and we were in the kitchen. I stepped up on a little two-foot stool to reach the top shelves in the kitchen cabinet. I had no idea Hutson was watching me until I stepped on that little stool and heard his little voice say, "Nana, are you allowed to do that?"

I guess not. My stool has been removed and in its place is a step ladder. Go figure!

> As for man, his days are like grass; he flourishes like a flower of the field; for the wind passes over it, and it is gone, and its place knows it no more (Psalm 103:15–16 ESV).

The scriptures are correct when life is compared to grass, here today and gone tomorrow. But even though physical abilities are limited as we age, we can still have a fulfilling life in Christ.

We older women recognize the unchanging love of our Father; we have experience. We know the importance of obeying His commandments. Help us to be active in teaching and mentoring children and young families. In gratitude for the many blessings the Lord has provided, we want to share and work. To help us navigate this aging process, please use us.

Discipleship does not end with old age.

The advice I would give to young people is this: You will have many earthly and eternal decisions to make. The practical financial decisions are earthly. They will stay here after we are gone. Your financial plans, wills, powers of attorneys for each other and for health care—don't put off the inevitable. Don't force the people you love most to make those decisions for you.

Your eternal decisions will go two ways: you will take them with you to heaven, and also leave them behind to live on in your children. Spend time with your family. Listen to them. Read to the children when they are young. Talk to them. Read Bible stories and eternal truths to them. When you do, you will be investing in "forever." Internalize this truth from Isaiah: "The grass withers, the flower fades, but the word of our God stands forever" (Isaiah 40:8).

Always remember, little eyes are watching you, so live truthful, loving lives before them. Show them God's love by your love. "As a father shows compassion to his children, so the Lord shows compassion to those who fear him" (Psalm 103:13 ESV). Little boys and girls soon become fathers and mothers who have learned from your actions how to treat others and their future spouses.

Husbands and wives, love God and each other above all else, and be thoughtful to everyone.

Growing old is stressful and peaceful. Growing old is sad and funny. Growing old loving God and others is the best life. I hope you continue choosing God as you age.

Most of all, remember the Lord's promise of compassion and love for you, your children, and your grandchildren as you show your fear and love for Him as you obey His precepts.

> But the steadfast love of the Lord is from everlasting to everlasting on those who fear him, and his righteousness to children's children, to those who keep his covenant and remember to do his commandments (Psalm 103:17–18 ESV).

Listen to My Life's Stories
by Laura Dayton

Communication at any age requires energy and brain power. This is particularly challenging when aging. Decades of information, experiences, and lessons are packed into our minds and blend together to formulate a lot of wisdom concerning the way to walk on the road of life. Current realities sometimes require effort and watchfulness that were never a consideration in younger years. What do I need as I age into this season of life? Most of the time, I simply need to be heard, and I'm not talking about the "uh huh" mantra. I'm talking about patient, engaged listening. It is one of the most respectful loving acts anyone can give to an older woman.

In mentoring women left alone, keep in mind that one thing they really miss is communication. Conversation sharpens their thinking, gives them a sense of connection, and is probably the most meaningful way to lift their hearts and help them feel the love we wish to convey. But older widows require a special kind of communication—something that is not necessarily needed in relationships with younger active sisters. Let me explain.

Communication can be particularly challenging for those who are aging. Consider their years of experiences and imagine how they stack up compared to yours. Godly older women have a treasure trove of wisdom to enable our walk on the road of life. So how does one access this wisdom from an older widow? Plan to slow down, sit down, and actively listen.

> **Plan to slow down, sit down, and actively listen.**

Jesus laid a foundation of understanding when He set forth some enlightenment concerning the quality of patient engaged listening. In Matthew 13:43, He concludes His teaching in story form by making a profound request: "He who has ears, let him hear!"

As with Jesus, many aging women tell stories. Why? Because they hold the meat and potatoes of life's best and worst choices. In them are the nuggets of happiness and warnings of unhappy consequences witnessed by decades of experience and observation. Auditory listening is not necessarily heart listening, as any mother training her little ones knows. A young mother recently stated, "It seems I say the same things over and over!" Even though clear consequences followed, she wondered, "Will they ever get it?" We used to refer to this as being a broken record. With time and persistence, children usually adjust their behaviors and attitudes when they have learned to hear a certain tone in their mothers' voices and directions.

Doesn't God also repeat His holy instructions over and over until we finally hear with our hearts and yield our stubborn wills to His? Perhaps that is why God recorded for all time the importance of listening to the instruction of older women who have lived reverent and good lives. We are to regard "older women as mothers, younger women as sisters with all purity. Honor widows who are really widows" (1 Timothy 5:2–3 NKJV).

And Titus 2 gives us the scope of older women's wisdom and instruction with descriptive words such as sober, reverent, temperate, sound in the faith, loving, patient, not slanderers or indulgent. Older women should teach good things. They have God's authority to admonish the young women to love their husbands, to love their children, to be discreet, chaste, homemakers, good, and obedient to their own husbands so as to bring honor to God. Perhaps we've heard these Titus 2 words over and over. But are we listening?

Recently when sharing a story with my daughter, she commented: "Mom, you told me that already!" "Why the repetition?" you may ask. Well, a good lesson is worth repeating. As in the early years of training the young, we need patience. Most of the time I get the ears but not the engagement that lets me know her hearing has met up with her head and heart. I am an aging broken record, but I know when my words have finally landed because I will hear one word from her: "Gotcha!"

I am an aging woman; be patient with my stories. Listen for the nuggets. Get to the "gotcha!" It will be a blessing for me and for you, the listener.

> Give attention to my words; incline your ear to my sayings. Do not let them depart from your sight; keep them in the midst of your heart (Proverbs 4:20–21).

A Final Charge

What a joy it has been to share with you, the reader, our thoughts on mentoring our sisters in the family of God. Christian women play many roles, and we hope we have challenged you in the role you are living right now. Always remember that we love you and are praying for you as you walk daily with our Lord.

Our grateful hearts go out to Betty Bender, Lea Fowler, Fran Carpenter, and Judith Merriam for seeing the necessity of women studying the Word of God together. We authors have personally received so many blessings because these four women established the practice of mentoring sisters. How many lives are still being touched as a result of their insight long ago in the beautiful Maine woods!

As we see in Titus 2, sisters helping sisters is a charge God has given us all. Wherever God has placed you, my sister, look for spiritual women with whom you can study or begin a "Love Circle." How important it is to leave a sacred legacy for our own daughters, physical and spiritual. In the process of their repeating this legacy, not only will Christian women mature in the faith, but God will be glorified. And that is what our effort is about in the first place.

Just as this book began by honoring our mentor, Betty Bender, it is appropriate to close with thoughts from her. Go back to page 13, and make the "Things I Learned from Betty" your own. She is gone now, but her memory lives on and her influence is playing out in our grandchildren. Imagine now that Betty is asking you, "Would you like to start a Love Circle in your home?" Pick up the mentoring baton and say with her, "I wake up each day determined to bring everyone I meet a little closer to the Lord."

Finally, make Psalm 37:4 your motto: "Delight yourself in the Lord; and He will give you the desires of your heart."

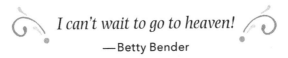

I can't wait to go to heaven!
—Betty Bender

Endnotes

Chapter 2

1. Todd Smith, "Ten Ways to Be a Good Listener," *Little Things Matter* (blog), March 3, 2010, http://www.littlethingsmatter.com/blog/2010/03/03/10-ways-to-being-a-good-listener1.

Chapter 5

1. William D. Mounce, *Pastoral Epistles, World Biblical Commentary*, Vol. 46 (Grand Rapids, MI: Zondervan, 2000), 397.

2. Supernanny, www.supernanny.co.uk.

3. "Christian Kids' Humor," accessed April 13, 2020, http://javacasa.com/humor/mouthsofbabes.htm.

Chapter 6

1. Judy Miller, *It Only Takes A Spark*. Used by permission. (Pasadena, TX: Dawn Publications, 1987), 15–16.

2. Sheila Keckler Butt, *No Greater Joy* (Huntsville, AL: Publishing Designs, Inc., 1999), 14.

3. Betty S. Bender, *To Love a Child* (Nashville, TN: 20th Century Christian, 1989), 141, 157.

4. Cris Rowan, contributor, "The Impact of Technology on the Developing Child," May 29, 2013, *HuffPost* (blog), https://www.huffpost.com/entry/technology-children-negative-impact_b_3343245.

5. "Young Parents' Prayer," *Inspirational Christian Stories and Poems*, Inspirational Archive.com, March 24, 2011, http://www.inspirationalarchive.com/276/young-parents-prayer/#ixzz3XPRdo390.

Chapter 7

1. Hodding Carter, *Where Main Street Meets the River* (New York: Rinehart & Company, 1953), 337.

2. *Adam Clark Commentary on Genesis*, Genesis 2:24, StudyLight.org, https://www.studylight.org/commentaries/acc/genesis-2.html.

3. *Matthew Henry's Complete Commentary on the Bible*, Section III, Genesis 2:21–25, studylight.org/commentaries/mhm/genesis-2.html.

4. Larry Deason, *Being Real* (Lady Lake, FL: Life Communications, 2005, theabidingword.com), 3. Free download at http://theabidingword.com/logos/LifeComm/LCL-BeingReal.pdf.

Chapter 8

1. Em, "If My Child Marries Yours," *Teach Me to Braid* (blog), September 27, 2014, teachmetobraid.blogspot.com/2014/09/if-my-child-marries-yours.html.

2. Fred H. Wight, *Manners and Customs of Bible Lands* (Moody Press, 1983), Chapter 14.

3. Dodinsky, *Good Reads Quotes*, https://www.goodreads.com/quotes/7513037-when -faced-with-senseless-drama-spiteful-criticisms-and-misguided-opinions.

Chapter 9

1. Patsy Loden, *Loving Your Husband* (Huntsville, AL: Publishing Designs, Inc., 2018), 229.

2. Loden, *Loving Your Husband*, 230.

Chapter 10

1. Lea Fowler, *Precious in the Sight of God* (Fort Worth, TX: Quality Publications, 1983), 8, 10.

2. Don McWhorter and Jane McWhorter, *Living Together in Knowledge* (Huntsville, AL: Publishing Designs, Inc., 2008), 34.

3. Loden, *Loving Your Husband*, 44.

Chapter 11

1. *Coffman's Commentaries on the Bible*, Mark 15:41, https://www.studylight.org /commentaries/bcc/mark-15.html.

2. Becky Blackmon, *Seek the Precious Moments* (Huntsville, AL: Publishing Designs, Inc., 2019), 222.

3. Becky Blackmon, *A Pearl Seeker* (Huntsville, AL: Publishing Designs, Inc., 2016), 184–185.

Chapter 12

1. Loden, *Loving Your Husband*, 228.

2. Brenda Poarch, *Side by Side* (Huntsville, AL: Publishing Designs, Inc., 2018), 49–50, 53.

Memorable Moments

Below: At a yearly Bible-study meeting, the writers took a break. This table scene is a witness to their diligence.

Above: Celebration photo 2019. Mentor Me *submitted to publisher; the future is bright!*

Betty Bender, Laura Dayton, Judy Cofer, Brenda Birckholtz, Martha Coletta, Becky Blackmon

Below: Betty Bender, Becky Blackmon, Judy Cofer

Below: Laura Dayton, Brenda Birckholtz, Betty Bender

Above: 2019: Martha Coletta, Laura Dayton, Judy Cofer, Brenda Birckholtz, Peggy Coulter (editor), Becky Blackmon.